The Mystery of the Missing Classic

By Eugene Brotzman

Copyright © 2010 Gene Brotzman, Prairie du Sac, Wisconsin.
Printed in the United States of America. Except as permitted under the United States Copyright Act of 1976, no part of this publication may be reproduced or distributed in any form or by any means, or stored in a database or retrieval system, without the prior written permission of the publisher.

ISBN: 978-0-9844413-4-1

Library of Congress Control #2010927053

This book is available at special quantity discounts. The author is available for personal appearances with Greenie the 1932 Plymouth Rumble Seat Coupe. Contact Eugene Brotzman at 608-643-0717 or brotzman1035@verizon.net.

Cover and interior design: Sarah White
Images from the collection of Gene Brotzman except where noted.

Printed in the United States.

This book is dedicated to all of the old car buffs who see the real history in an old car and want to preserve it just as it was when it was manufactured. Nothing thrills me more than to see a very old car, either in its original state, or restored to its original state. Such dignity and character.

You can recognize a true old car buff. He's the one who can name an old car's manufacturer on first sight. Just try that with the new cars of today.

Contents

Acknowledgments iii
Introduction. v

Part 1: The Crime

Chapter 1: From Classic Beauty to a
          Frankenstein Fix-Up—1932–1967 3
Chapter 2: The Scene of the Crime 17
Chapter 3: Fire! 29
Chapter 4: The Mystery of the Missing Classic . . . 41

Part 2: The Pursuit

Chapter 5: Hot on the Trail 51
Chapter 6: The Scene of the Real Crime 65

i

Chapter 7: A Race Against Time 73
Chapter 8: Voluntary Clues. 85

Part 3: The Recovery

Chapter 9: In the Nick of Time 101
Chapter 10: The Advocate's Last Challenge—
      Restoration 115

Epilogue: Leaving a Trail of Classic Delight—
      Greenie's New Life 133
Appendix I: Relationships 143
Appendix II: Sources for Parts and Information . . 145

About the Author. 149

Acknowledgments

Author and editor, Sarah White of Madison, Wisconsin, has been a constant source of help and inspiration to me during the writing and completion of this project. My heart felt thanks, Sarah, for your very capable work. Your experience with writing editing proved to be invaluable.

While I wrote the manuscript in the first person, Sarah felt it best to be written in the third person. She did a great job in converting the text to the third person. Places in the book referring to me in glowing terms we will have to downplay. I do not wish to convey the impression that I am seeking to put myself on a pedestal.

Ken's Classics, the restoration shop, did a great job in restoring the coupe. Ken Stadele was very accommodating during the gathering of information. Ken went so far as to give Sarah White a tour of the facility located at Muscoda, Wisconsin. I have the highest regard for Ken and his crew who restored the coupe to mint condition.

Greg Nelson, the former owner of the coupe, was most helpful in providing background information, which included the amateur restoration with his dad, Glenn Nelson. Greg's mom, Bonnie Nelson, provided the photo that was instrumental in locating and recovering the coupe. Thanks to both Greg and Bonnie.

The Eau Claire Museum loaned their well-informed Frank Smoot to help with the social history of Eau Claire during the 1970s. Frank was extremely helpful in uncovering vital information about Eau Claire. Many thanks for your help, Frank. The staff of the Eau Claire Leader-Telegram were also helpful in the book's research. Several of the attorneys involved contributed their perspectives, which we appreciate.

Thanks to all of my family and friends who encouraged me to write the whole story of the 1932 Plymouth RS Coupe, rather than just telling the story.

My heartfelt gratitude to my lovely wife, Barbara M. Hoyum Brotzman, who so patiently put up with my typing on the word processor and leaving other tasks till later. My 30 years of marriage to Barb has been a dream come true.

Introduction

This true account of a 1932 Plymouth PA rumble seat coupe with dual side-mount tires is not only factual, but is a most unusual tale of deception, dishonesty and downright theft. The setting is Eau Claire, Wisconsin, a city of about 70,000 permanent residents at the time the events recorded here take place—the years 1974 through 1978. Although I tell the story mostly in the third person, I am the one who experienced every detail of the story, primarily because the antique coupe belonged to me.

This book is a memoir and as such, relies on my memory of events that occurred long ago, assisted by the extensive files I kept throughout the events as they unfolded. While I have made use of those files in writing the *Mystery of the Missing Classic*, the conclusions drawn are largely dependent on my memory. I make no claim to knowledge of the laws that might apply to this case or the customary conduct of legal proceedings. I have only described what I saw, felt, heard, and did, and what I understood of the actions of others.

Why did it take me thirty years to write this riveting account? First, I must tell you what it was like to have such a unique story hanging over my head, but I

The Mystery of the Missing Classic

was doing nothing about it. Many times I was asked to tell the story to individuals or to groups. A classic example occurred just last Tuesday evening. My wife, Barbara, and I were at some friends home for a birthday party of an old lady of 83. The gentleman of the home told a brief story of having a monkey for a pet when he was a kid.

Upon finishing his story, he then said, "And now I am going to do something not in my usual manner, I am going to call on Gene Brotzman to tell you of the experience with his '32 Plymouth coupe, even though he does not know that I am going to make this request of him." While I was surprised by the request, I am always prepared to tell the story because the experiences are still so real in my life. Sitting in a large rocking chair, with 30-plus adults gathered around me, I spent the next 25 minutes telling just the highlights. All eyes stayed glued on me as the story unfolded. Following my abridged account, I was surrounded by smiles, handshakes, and compliments. All wanted a copy of my book upon completion.

So why had I waited 30 years to put in writing what was so familiar to me and so interesting to others? I knew how to write the facts of the experience, but I allowed everything else to take precedence over my desire to turn this story into a book. Besides, I had not taken

Introduction

time to explore sources of help in putting my writing into book form and to get it printed. Procrastination was really the name of the game for me.

Seven years ago I was diagnosed with multiple myeloma cancer. It was then I came to the conclusion that if my story got into print it was now or never. It was in June of 2009 that I came into contact with author and editor Sarah White of Madison, Wisconsin. Sarah graciously consented to help me with the project. I settled in to my word processor and found writing the story was enjoyable. Sarah took over to edit and "tweak" the manuscript, design the cover, and prepare the book for printing. She has been great with which to work.

This true story tells of a 72-year-old lady stealing the 1932 Plymouth Coupe and the ensuing search for the car. It is bound to capture your interest and attention as you imagine yourself in the same situations and decide how you might have handled them.

Depending on the uncertain future, I may be given time to write of my many experiences while serving 38 years as an elementary and middle school principal, and serving with the US army two years in Korea during the Korean War.

I've found the joy in authorship. I hope you find joy in reading my work.

— Gene Brotzman, March 2010

The Mystery of the Missing Classic

Part 1: The Crime

The Mystery of the Missing Classic

"The Smoothness of an Eight: The Economy of a Four" – Advertising for the new coupe began appearing in national magazines in 1931.

Chapter 1:
From Classic Beauty to a
Frankenstein Fix-Up—1932–1967

This is the story of a plucky little Plymouth that survived the Depression, went on a honeymoon, disappeared into long years of obscurity, emerged in the 1960s to be badly patched together, and then suffered a mysterious and intriguing car-napping—seized by a landlady with no apparent appreciation for its value, and hidden for years in sad neglect.

It's also the story of a persistent advocate who ultimately saved this lovely vehicle in distress.

If you love classic beauty in an automobile and appreciate a good mystery story, meet the "little green car"—a 1932 Plymouth PA Rumble Seat Coupe. We'll call her Greenie.

The Mystery of the Missing Classic

Greenie's Pedigree

In the giant poker game that is the automotive industry, Chrysler held a handful of aces with the PA... still a much sought-after vehicle.
(James Benjaminson. *Plymouth Bulletin*, 152.)

Greenie came from a distinguished family. The Plymouth PA was a breakthrough automobile. The rumble seat coupe was one of 11 models offered in this extraordinary accomplishment from the darkest days of the Great Depression. Walter Chrysler took a considerable gamble, spending $2.5 million to bring out a top-quality competitor in the low-cost car market just when others were cutting back.

The PA series became so highly regarded that it catapulted Plymouth into third place in sales even when its overall production was a fraction of its competitors, Chevy and Ford. Even Franklin Delano Roosevelt owned a Plymouth PA Phaeton, a four-door convertible with the same engineering breakthroughs that made all Plymouth PAs so desirable, so "sought-after."

Greenie was particularly sought after—but for reasons we'll explore as the mystery unfolds. The mystery itself is made more compelling by the fact that the PA was, and still is, so highly valued. Here's the low-down on the most fetching features of this extraordinary line of automobiles.

Chapter 1

A Nov. 29, 1933 pose shows President Franklin D. Roosevelt wearing a hat, and his Plymouth's top is a mess. [World Wide Photos]. Reprinted with permission from the Plymouth Bulletin, *vol. 42, #6, September–October 2001.*

The major innovation was an improved method of mounting the engine called "Floating Power." Until this breakthrough, economical four-cylinder autos vibrated way too much for comfort, much more than six- or eight-cylinder models. For the PA, Chrysler engineers almost entirely eliminated vibration by mounting the engine following its center of gravity and cushioning it in a floating "rubber sandwich" system. This Plymouth exclusive was soon widely imitated—but before that, it earned Chrysler the right to advertise the "Smoothness of an Eight and the Economy of a Four."

The Mystery of the Missing Classic

On *Oct 10, 1931, the* Saturday Evening Post *carried Chrysler's ad promoting the Plymouth's record-breaking run exactly two months plus a day following its completion. Reprinted with permission from the* Plymouth Bulletin, *vol. 42, #6, September–October 2001.*

Chapter 1

Torture Testing: How the PA Earned the Right to Boast

- Everything Chrysler boasted about in advertising, the PA earned from testing.
- To prove that the car was fire- and crash-proof, Plymouth engineers in Detroit took a PA sedan to nearby Bald Mountain, a natural area with the steepest hills and most rugged terrain in southeastern Michigan. They pushed the car over a cliff. The car overturned, tumbled, and crashed downward—and landed upright on its wheels, not a window broken! The engineers promptly started it up and drove it to the top, pushing it over a total of 19 times. After that experiment, they drove off with a few dents as the only consequence. Repairs cost $50. Marketers felt justified in calling it a "Triumph of Engineering."
- To prove its durability, engineers took the PA to Death Valley to endure extreme heat, then on to Mt. Wilson to endure extreme cold. Successful both times.
- Driven by a 57-year-old Chrysler employee, the PA broke all existing transcontinental speed records in a run from San Francisco to New York and back.
- Plymouth engineers took the car to some of the nation's largest cities where they asked each of the mayors to ride blindfolded in the car and guess if it ran on four or eight cylinders. The clear majority said it felt like an eight—another justification for the slogan "The smoothness of an eight and the economy of a four."

7

The Mystery of the Missing Classic

In addition to the competitive advantages of Floating Power, Plymouth had the jump on Chevy and Ford in both design and materials. The frame of the new PA was the "double drop" type, which lowered the car's center of gravity—the center part of the frame—allowing the body to sit lower. The overall height went down to 67 inches (64" on the roadster model), making the Plymouth look longer than its modest 169-inch length. So, it not only looked snazzier than the competition, it held the road better. The PA's designers also eliminated structural wood. Each body was welded into a solid unit from five steel sections, beginning with a full steel floor pan. This made the car "fire and crash proof," according to the factory.

The PA was also a powerful little speedster. Propelled by a 196.1 cid, 56-horsepower L-head four, its high-turbulence Silver Dome cylinder head gave the PA increased pep; it could go from 0 to 40 miles per hour in only 9.7 seconds.

Another PA advantage was its "Easy-Shift" transmission with a "silent" second gear. Second and high gear were in constant mesh, allowing the driver to upshift or downshift without double-clutching. Coupled to the rear of this transmission was a cam-and-roller unit that allowed the driver to shift between gears without any use of the clutch. This feature was known as

Chapter 1

"Free Wheeling." It was not new in the market, but Plymouth was the only low-cost auto to adopt it.

Some critics thought Free Wheeling was unsafe because it put a strain on the brakes. Once again, Plymouth outdid the competition. It was the only line of cars to use a hydraulic brake system, which used brake fluid in lines from the master (main) cylinder to the wheel cylinders to activate the brakes. The competitors lagged behind, saddled with the old mechanical, cable-actuated system.

The PA was the first Plymouth to use a built-in radiator grille, and its vertical radiator louvres could be finished in chrome rather than paint. The radiator was situated forward enough to require a longer hood. This added to the long look of what was a truly stylish automobile. The unique oval rear window was only one of the design features that led the advertisers to claim the PA was "the most beautiful low-priced car in the world."

Capping the PA's fashion achievements was the stunning hand-sculptured, finely detailed "Flying Lady" radiator cap, which added to its beauty and became a symbol for the PA's record-breaking cross-country trip. The Flying Lady was designed by Avard T. Fairbanks, head of the sculpture department at the University of Michigan, Ann Arbor.

Fairbanks needed a new car but it was the Depression and he couldn't afford one. He sought out the nearby Chrysler Corporation and negotiated a design for their PA radiator cap in return for a free car. He based his design on the idea of "Floating Power," the key distinction used in the company's advertising.

Fairbanks designed a mermaid based on the little mermaid of Norse mythology, coming up out of a swirling wave and bearing eagle's wings. The Flying Lady was a smashing success from the time she appeared. Her contours may have had something to do with her widespread popularity. People acknowledged her graceful appearance mimicking motion, the feathery pattern on her wings, her flowing wavy hair, but everyone talked about the lovely lady's "healthy torso." Fairbanks dismissed the fuss with this simple statement: "She's a mermaid, and that's just how mermaids are!" (*Plymouth Bulletin* 246, (Jan–Feb 2001) He got his reward in a handsome red 1932 Chrysler Royal Eight, definitely not from the low-cost end of the scale.

For devoted motorheads, there's a lot more to say about the PA's style and engineering innovations. (See James Benjaminson's article on the PA in issue 152 of the *Plymouth Bulletin* for more details and specifications.) Only 9,696 of the 1932 PA Rumble Seat Coupe were made. But even without more details, Greenie's elevated value as a rare member of the PA family should

Chapter 1

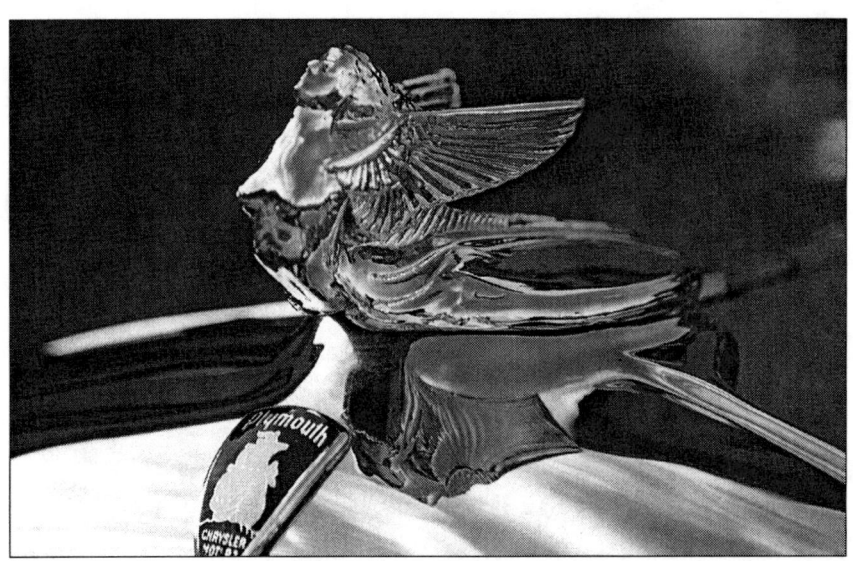

The Flying Lady Radiator Cap. Photo by Thomas Glatch. Reprinted with permission from Collectible Automobile, *October 1995.*

be clear by now.

Walter Chrysler surely knew the value of his big gamble. There's a story many historians tell—after first noting that it's not exactly substantiated yet. As the story goes, Walter was on hand when the first PAs rolled off the assembly line in 1931. Remembering the discouraging words he'd heard from Henry Ford, he hopped into the third car off the line and drove it to nearby Dearborn, Michigan where he presented it to Henry and his son Edsel. After Walter enjoyed watching them look it over, he handed Henry the keys and took a taxi home.

Knowing the historical significance of Greenie's

pedigreed family intensifies the mystery of Greenie's car-napping. Imagine the loss felt by an informed collector when in 1976 he discovered that poor Greenie had seemingly disappeared!

Greenie's Lucky First Owner

We can't be absolutely sure of Greenie's first owner, but indications point to Mrs. Lila Olson Neuhaus of Onalaska, Wisconsin. She bought a '32 green Plymouth PA Rumble Seat Coupe new at Leitchfield's garage in Eau Claire before Easter in 1932. She was teaching in Augusta, Wisconsin at the time. When she married in 1937, she and her husband drove Greenie on their honeymoon. Not surprisingly, by the summer of 1939 a larger car seemed appropriate and Mrs. and Mr. Neuhaus traded Greenie in on a '36 Buick at Strieke Motor Company in LaCrosse, Wisconsin. Greenie had been with Lila for seven years.

In a letter that arrived during the race to recover Greenie, Lila reported: "The last we knew of our little green car was that someone from Coon Valley, Wisconsin was driving it."

The Lost Years

Coon Valley? Doesn't that sound like the last stop on the road to obscurity? It was. We don't see Greenie

Chapter 1

Mrs. Lila Olson Neuhaus with brother and sister in front of her automobile. Photo courtesy of Lila Neuhaus.

again until 1964. She must have gone through horrible experiences—the kind that belong in a movie about the down-and-out decline of an elegant aristocrat. Please, draw a curtain over any such imaginings. Just think of this time between 1939 and 1964 as the lost years. The truth is tough enough.

Glenn Nelson of West Salem, Wisconsin called Greenie "a basket case" when he found her in 1964. The unnamed former owner had taken it apart, intending to put it back together with parts that weren't worn, rusted, or defective. Apparently he lost enthusiasm for the task. That's the shape the little car was in when Glenn found out about it and bought what might have been a pile of parts. He set out with his teenage son Greg to restore it.

The Nelsons' Fix-Up

Unfortunately Glenn Nelson was a pure amateur. If that weren't enough to promise a shaky restoration, Glenn didn't start until 1965 and he died in 1967. The Nelsons were living in Eau Claire, Wisconsin at the time Glenn started working on Greenie. It was to a large extent a project to share with his son Greg, who was nearing driving age. "You're going to have to earn the right to drive," said Glenn, indicating that ownership of the fixer-upper would be Greg's reward.

The two needed some kind of reconciliation. Glenn was—to be blunt—a man typical of his time and place, a drinker of much coffee and alcohol, a big smoker, and the kind of guy who related to his son with commands rather than conversation.

Greg recalls feeling fine about working on the vintage car, although he characterizes himself as "a '60s muscle-car kid." He and Glenn worked on Greenie for a couple years in their garage. "The car was a lot of fun to work on," says Greg. "That was a simple engine."

The more he worked on it, the more his interest in auto mechanics grew. But Glenn's drinking worsened. Greg moved out of the family home when he finished high school. He and his dad had been fighting. But working on Greenie, the battered car, was a bright spot between them. Greg ultimately valued Greenie as the

Chapter 1

best memory he had of his dad. Glenn Nelson died at the age of 41 in 1967.

Maybe what they did was good for their relationship. Maybe it even raised poor Greenie from a basket case. But from a collector's point of view, Greenie had become a functional Frankenstein.

- Headlights were from a Model A Ford.
- The front bumper was from a 1931 Chevrolet.
- The single tail light was a reproduction from a Napa Parts store.
- The hubcaps were original but in poor condition.
- The Claxon horn was mounted on the front headlight bar rather than under the hood.
- The radiator cap was generic, no Flying Lady in sight.
- The upholstery was covered with black vinyl (probably Naugahyde).
- The dash was brush-painted green to match the exterior.
- The interior left window frame was missing, as was the oval window crank handle.
- The engine ran well, but the radiator shell was mounted improperly, causing the radiator cap to be raised, which allowed fluid to escape.
- The rumble seat cushions were covered with black vinyl.

So Greenie became an inheritance. Glenn's wife and Greg's mother, Bonnie June Nelson, later signed the car over to Greg, a shy person with no idea of what to do with his life. Greg in turn signed over the money and home his dad had left in his name to his mother, who was too ill to work.

Greg started college at the University of Wisconsin–Eau Claire in 1968. He soon realized he didn't know why he was there, participating in those torrid days of drugs, sex, and rock 'n' roll, going to school to avoid the draft. He quit to work in gas stations where he could pursue the interest he'd developed while working on Greenie. "Playing" with cars suited him. But then, in that same year 1968, he was drafted.

Poor Greenie was left once again to languish while Greg went off to Vietnam.

Chapter 2: The Scene of the Crime

Yes, there was a crime committed against Greenie… and it happened in Eau Claire, Wisconsin. She disappeared in 1974.

But first, Greenie got to tool around a bit. She became Greg Nelson's "girl magnet" sometime after Greg's father Glenn died in 1967. Greg valued the car even though he thought of himself as more of a muscle-car kind of guy. He was drafted in 1968, and went to Vietnam in the infantry. Like so many other veterans, he has little to say about it, except that he was a "grunt" while there. Vietnam was a highly unpopular war, and Greg had some bad experiences coming home in his uniform. It was years before he would get together with friends made while in the service and compare notes on their symptoms of post-traumatic stress disorder.

The Mystery of the Missing Classic

Greenie's first restoration—functional, but a Frankenstein.

Greg returned from Vietnam in 1970. Shortly after that, he met Mary Lou Urban at a ballroom in Bloomer, Wisconsin and dated her for a couple years. They married in 1972, and Greenie got to be part of the family right from the start. When the couple visited Mary Lou's folks in Bloomer, they made the drive in Greenie.

Shortly after their marriage, Greg and Mary Lou moved to 508½ Vine Street in Eau Claire, the scene of the crime. They kept their four-year old Ford outside and Greenie got the garage. That's the spot from which Greenie disappeared. To trace the mystery of her disappearance, we need to take a closer look at what it was

Chapter 2

like for the young newlyweds to be living in Eau Claire in the early 1970s.

At Home in Eau Claire, Wisconsin

Do you remember the early 1970s? The demonstrations? The escalation of the Vietnam war into Cambodia and Laos? The shootings at Kent State and Jackson State? The Watergate scandal? The impeachment of President Richard Nixon? The famous "generation gap"? Those were tense years.

In cities around the country, the early 1970s saw the beginning of what has come to be known as the culture wars between defenders of the establishment and advocates for change. Historically this isn't an unusual split, but now, at the end of the first decade of the 21st century, the unresolved split has become a chasm. While the current shape of the conflict is primarily political, it began back in the early 1970s as an intense conflict between authority and young rebels against authority, people over 30 against people under 30, the culture versus the counterculture—straights and hippies as some would call them.

This tension between established authority and the young is relevant to our story because the mystery's two main characters occupied opposite sides of the split. So, how did Eau Claire fare in the first years of the culture

The Mystery of the Missing Classic

An Eau Claire "Town Meeting '76" was one of several events during the Bicentennial Year. At the meeting, several hundred residents gathered to discuss problems and alternatives in planning for the future of Eau Claire and the surrounding area. Photo from "Our Story," a special bicentennial publication, courtesy of the Eau Claire Leader Telegram.

wars? Let's look at a little history to see the roots of the Eau Claire "establishment."

Eau Claire, meaning "clear water," is located at the confluence of the Chippewa and Eau Claire rivers in

20

Chapter 2

the Chippewa Valley. It once was dense with magnificent white pines, huge and tempting trees that fed the growth of Eau Claire as a lumbering town—nicknamed Sawdust City until 1910 when the last of the pines floated downriver. Until the mid 1960s when the interstate highways appeared, Eau Claire depended largely on its rich opportunities for farmers. From the 1920s to the 1980s Eau Claire's primacy in the dairy industry made it the center for calculating U.S. milk prices—prices were based on a producer's geographical distance from Eau Claire.

In the 1970s Eau Claire boomed. Property tax values went up 25% in the late 1960s and another 25% in the early 1970s. The campus of the University of Wisconsin–Eau Claire bulged with 28 new buildings constructed between 1960 and 1975. By the late 1970s the Eau Claire metropolitan area was among the 25 fastest-growing metro areas in the country. The interstate highway arrived in the mid-1960s, providing new opportunities for attracting multi-state industries and for trucking. Small 100- to 200-employee industries appeared in healthy numbers, and blue-collar employment grew due to large manufacturers like Uniroyal Tire and National Presto Industries. Mechanization on farms reduced the number of people needed to run a farm and sent a small migration of workers into Eau

The Mystery of the Missing Classic

Claire to help with the industrial boom.

But the years of the 1970s also saw both the advantages of growth and the pain that comes during periods of transition. Transitions create hard times for people who are dedicated to the establishment but who don't or can't keep up with the times. And the transition of the 1970s was particularly difficult because of open conflict between those who feared the look of the future and those who grooved on growth and change.

Urban renewal in the 1960s did away with the city's old-fashioned main street. By 1970, when Greg came back from Vietnam, most of the two-story commercial buildings that characterized the downtown, including a gorgeous Richardson Romanesque department store, had been torn down and replaced by bunker-style architecture. In 1971 a 55,000-square-foot enclosed shopping mall came to the south of town. Long-established downtown businesses either moved to the mall or tried to hang on as the downtown declined.

In 1970, planners thought metropolitan Eau Claire represented a new kind of city emerging in the United States called the dispersed or "cluster" city. These clusters resulted from new highway systems connecting major centers of employment, trade, services, and manufacturing. Feeder roads tied rural areas to these centers. Planners believed cluster cities would account for almost all non-farm growth in the Upper Midwest between 1970–2000. Eau Claire's population in 1970 reached 67,000 and was projected to top 100,000 by 1985. (Today it still hasn't reached that number.)

Optimism ruled in some quarters, while in others tension mounted over the rapid pace of all the new-fangled this and that, over hippies and welfare cheats, long hair and laziness.

Goodbye to the Eau Claire of the 1950s

The Establishment in Eau Claire, like almost every place in the U.S.A., was based on the values associated with the 1950s. Those were glory days for Eau Claire as a baseball-loving All-American city. In 1952 the Eau Claire Bears, a Minor League team connected to the Major League Boston Braves, hired Henry Aaron from the Negro League. Aaron, who was to become a Baseball Hall of Fame legend, was 18 years old and about to enter a white world for the first time from his home in Mobile, Alabama.

"Henry Aaron couldn't have landed in a better city than Eau Claire if he wanted to experience Middle America," says Jerry Poling in his book, *A Summer Up North: Henry Aaron and the Legend of Eau Claire Baseball.* Poling presents Eau Claire as a middle-class, Midwestern town, safe and scenic. Ann Landers and Abi-

The Mystery of the Missing Classic

The statue of Henry Aaron is the centerpiece of a pedestrian plaza outside Carson Park baseball stadium, which was remodeled in the 1990s. Photo by Jerry Poling (employed by the Eau Claire Press Company, publisher of the Leader-Telegram*). Photo courtesy of the* Leader-Telegram*.*

Chapter 2

gail Van Buren—not yet known as Dear Ann and Dear Abby—lived in Eau Claire from the mid 1940s to the mid 1950s.

But among celebrities, Henry Aaron is clearly Eau Claire's heartthrob. In 1994 the city unveiled a bronze statue of Aaron outside the beloved old WPA-built baseball stadium at Carson Park. "It was a blessed day for me," Aaron said in later years. "A lot of things happened to me in my 23 years as a ballplayer, but nothing touched me more than that day in Eau Claire."

The Times Are A-Changin'

The Eau Claire Bears became the Eau Claire Braves in 1954 and played their final game in 1962. Fan interest had waned. By the late 1960s, without doubt the 1950s—and all that those years stood for—were gone for good except as a glossy memory among those who resisted social change.

Eau Claire managed better than some to keep its cool during the transitional upheavals of the 1960s and 1970s. It's not a place where tensions come to the surface, it's a "Norwegian" kind of place like Garrison Keillor's imaginary Lake Wobegone. Nonetheless, the tensions did exist and they popped out in personal, daily discord between citizens of the old guard and the heedless young. In 1974 when Henry Aaron broke Babe

The Mystery of the Missing Classic

Ruth's lifetime home run record playing for the Atlanta Braves, Eau Claire took note from afar, but was about as socially repressed and divided as it ever got. And in that same year, Greenie disappeared.

> **A Sensible Sort of City**
>
> Historian Frank Smoot of Eau Claire recalls an incident that illustrates how courtesy ruled in Eau Claire when it was sensibly applied to a population willing to avoid confronting its tensions. At the time of the Kent State shooting in 1970, about 150 students from UW–Eau Claire staged a protest at Chancellor Haas's home. Mrs. Haas, a "tiny little intelligent woman" invited them in for hot chocolate and constructive conversation. "That's how protest goes in Eau Claire," says Mr. Smoot, "We're mad as heck…but a cup of hot chocolate will do for now."

In the 1970s, Eau Claire thought of itself as a hard-working, productive, blue collar town, but it was really one of many "middle America" places where those who believed in "my country right or wrong" were becoming the seething "silent majority," and the young and progressive were becoming the counterculture. The

Chapter 2

emotional gap between adult and youth grew, particularly as the enrollment at the University of Wisconsin-Eau Claire exploded. The University grew crowded but it remained disconnected from the life of the town.

The students would come down to the Campus Tavern on Water Street, a working class bar in a blue-collar town. The workers drank inside the bars, while college kids partied outside, littering the downtown with trash to greet the "taxpaying citizens" on their way to Sunday morning church.

In Eau Claire the young were automatically considered counterculture—political and apolitical students alike, beer-drinking rowdies, young working class townies, young Vietnam vets, any young person who looked scruffy—all of them were considered counterculture. The District Attorney in Eau Claire considered Greg Nelson "disreputable" without knowing anything about him except that he was under 25.

"What," you might ask, "had Greg Nelson, Greenie's owner, to do with the DA of Eau Claire?" Well, now that you know something of the atmosphere in Eau Claire during the early 1970s, you can imagine what happened when young Greg Nelson—hair just over his ears, dressed in jeans, a working-class kid turned college student—came up against his landlady, Mrs. Olga Norbey, a property-owning, solid citizen

The Mystery of the Missing Classic

born in Norway in 1902 and 72 years old in 1974. Keep that image in mind as we arrive at the fateful day that launched the mystery of a missing classic. Back we go to March 24, 1974.

Chapter 3: Fire!

Eau Claire police officer Alan Lowry was patrolling the streets on a chilly Sunday afternoon, March 24, 1974, when he noticed smoke billowing out from under the eaves at 508½ Vine Street. He immediately called the fire department and then helped 85-year-old Martha Martin evacuate her half of the duplex shared with Greg and Mary Lou Nelson. The Nelsons were not at home.

By the time the fire department arrived, smoke was thick and pouring out from all sides of the one-and-a-half story frame building. Firefighter Bob Anderson donned an air mask and entered the Nelsons' apartment where, sad to say, he found their puppy Rascal laid out behind the couch. Anderson worked for 15 minutes trying to revive Rascal, but failed.

This was just the first blow in a barrage of bad

In 2009 the house on Vine Street, appearing shabby and hard-used, was for sale.

luck for the financially strapped Nelsons. And where, you might ask, was the young couple on that Sunday in March? Certainly not out having fun. They left the apartment at 6:00 in the morning. Mary Lou went to work at Sacred Heart Hospital, where she was a ward secretary in charge of patient records. Greg was doing duty on the picket-line at the Packerland Company in Chippewa Falls. Greenie, you'll be relieved to learn, sat safely in the detached garage up the alley behind 508½ Vine St.

Greg picked up Mary Lou after work and the two found fire trucks in their yard when they returned to

Chapter 3

their apartment. "It was a shack," said Greg Nelson many years later, referring to that apartment. It was one half of a duplex in a neighborhood of older homes and older residents. The hospital and the university were nearby. The apartment had two rooms upstairs, one room and a tacked-on kitchen addition downstairs. The kitchen was cold and so poorly insulated that ice crept two feet up the outside wall in winter. The pipes froze regularly. There was no central heating, just an old-fashioned parlor stove to heat the whole place.

Although the Nelsons had no renter's insurance, Greg didn't miss much of their belongings except the puppy. "If you don't have much, you don't lose much," he observed.

Now the Mystery Begins

In the mystery of Greenie's disappearance, there are many examples of strange and inexplicable motives, inertia, lazy information, possible deception, outright lies, and just plain blank spots. What should have been no more than a sad story became a race to discover the truth.

The first puzzle was why no one who was involved in the search for the truth—and for Greenie—seemed to know what caused the fire. It wasn't uncovered by any of the many lawyers who would be involved in tracing Greenie's disappearance. It appears that Mrs. Olga Jensen Norbey, the landlady, and her representatives believed it was a space heater. That's what Greg Nelson was told. But Greg was also told the official fire department report listed the fire as having an "undetermined origin." And yet on Monday, March 25, *the day after the fire*, the *Eau Claire Leader-Telegram* came out with an article describing the full details.

> Deputy Chief Delbert Ziebell reported the fire started in an overstuffed chair in the downstairs living room. It burned down through the floor and then across the floor to a north interior wall. The blaze then burned up the wall into an enclosed attic area. …Ziebell said the fire had been burning for some time and had burned through the studs and up through the wall bypassing the second floor bedroom area occupied by the Nelsons. Firemen were forced to cut into the roof and siding in the attic area to get at the blaze."

Greg and Mary Lou were probably too busy looking for a place to live to have seen the newspaper story, but why didn't Mrs. Norbey and all the lawyers say anything about the details described by the newspaper story? Those details probably wouldn't have weakened

Chapter 3

Norbey's case against Greg as the cause of the fire.

It's all but certain that Mrs. Olga Jensen Norbey collected insurance on the $20,000 worth of damage done to her building. And yet, she seized Greenie, claiming the car was compensation for Greg starting the fire. She and her representatives never used the newspaper story to back up their assertions. She filed no legal claim and she never had possession of Greenie's title. She simply locked Greenie in the garage to begin with … and then Greenie disappeared!

The Kid and the Landlady

So here we have our two lead characters: Greg Nelson and Olga Jensen Norbey, the scruffy young man and the elderly solid citizen, the perfect match-up to represent the hidden culture clash of the early 1970s. Of course there was no real face-to-face confrontation. Since renting the apartment Greg had dealt only with Mrs. Norbey's brother James. Greg did bump into Olga Norbey one time when she was cleaning up the apartment mess after the fire. That's when she informed him that the '32 Plymouth PA Rumble Seat Coupe was hers.

Greg had delayed in coming to get Greenie from the garage in the alley behind the burnt-out apartment on Vine St. It had taken him and Mary Lou five weeks to find a new place to live and to raise the security deposit

33

they needed. Friends helped them out in the meantime. When Greg went to retrieve Greenie, accompanied by his friend Robert Gabriel, he found the garage chained and locked.

Did Greg go to the law for help? Well, yes, after a time he did. He didn't hold a lot of hope. He felt powerless just being who he was. As he put it, "When a kid walks in to the cops to go up against a tax-paying, multiple-property-owning landlord—who would you vote for to win out?"

Perhaps his assessment was not so far from the reality of things in those days and in that city. After all, when Greg finally did seek help and went to the District Attorney, he got the cold shoulder. The DA told him that recovering the car would have to be done as a civil court case, but the district attorney's office didn't handle civil cases. "Get a lawyer," said the DA to Greg. (The DA would comment later that Greg looked disreputable.)

He might as well have told Greg to walk over the Alps. The poor guy had next to nothing to his name. He was up against a struggle for the basic necessities of life. How could he even imagine walking into some oak-paneled lawyer's office, let alone going there to hire one? He simply couldn't afford to get Greenie back.

On the other hand, did Mrs. Norbey have a plan

Chapter 3

for what to do with a car she had no title to? She later described the car as a junker. Was she unaware of its value? Actually, she and Greg both seemed to have strange blank spots in their dealings with each other—motiveless reactions, hapless inaction, and irrational claims. We must, at this point, leave Greenie tucked away somewhere and take a closer look at these two inexplicable protagonists.

There are reasons why Greg Nelson was so slow in trying to recover Greenie. Advice from the uncooperative district attorney was the only advice he got, and even before he went to Vietnam, Greg was not exactly a take-the-bull-by-the-horns go-getter. He was very much one of the guys, hanging out, well-liked, drifting a little—only, he was also a bit shy and a bit worn down by his early experiences under his hard-drinking dad. We can only imagine what Vietnam did to him. So many vets from that war just slipped into the cracks that splintered the life of the country. But Greg did not. His marriage in 1972 to Mary Lou put him on a more productive track than many of his fellow vets.

Greg's socializing after the marriage was almost entirely with Mary Lou's family outside Chippewa Falls near the village of Tilden. In the past he had gone to his own family's gatherings at his grandmother's farm outside Eleva, south of Eau Claire and east of Mondovi. The family set up card tables, drank beer, and played canasta. The gatherings tapered off when Greg's grandmother died in 1965. It was at these gatherings that Greg met his Aunt Dorris, who had married Gene Brotzman.

Dorris was Glenn Nelson's sister. Her husband, Gene, was a teacher and an elementary school principal. Greg admired Gene for his education and his demeanor. Gene, as you will soon learn, became Greenie's advocate, the man who sought the little green coupe's liberation. Gene was, perhaps, an inspiration to Greg, because after his marriage Greg went back to the university to become a school teacher. For three years he worked a minimum wage job for 54 hours a week while he went to school full time.

Greg worked at Hudson's Garage six days a week, including 3:00 p.m. to midnight on Fridays and returning at 6:00 a.m. on Saturday to open. When other people his age were out partying, Greg was at work, or studying, or both. He had the GI Bill for tuition and books, but he and Mary Lou struggled to make ends meet, particularly after the fire when they had to start all over again.

Eventually, Greg found he wasn't cut out to be a teacher. Rather than continue his schooling with no

Chapter 3

clear goal in mind, he left. He joined the National Guard for the money it brought in and got a job cutting meat at Packerland Packing of Chippewa Falls. The young couple had no children. Greg thought long and hard about that. He feared the effects of Agent Orange that he was exposed to in Vietnam and how that could affect any offspring.

Greg Nelson was no match for the formidable Olga Norbey. Olga was not a powerhouse in Eau Claire, but she had standing as a long-time property owner and landlady. She was a senior citizen, married to LeRoy Norbey, a technician at Benson Optical in Eau Claire. Her attorney, G., was perhaps the most influential lawyer in town; his firm was the largest in the city. We will hear more about him in the coming chapters.

In any case both Greg and his Uncle Gene, the advocate, were convinced that Mrs. Norbey had enough influence to load the odds against them. She did have influence as a solid citizen, and she was, as one lawyer put it, "a picture of the sweet little old lady." But most evidence does not reveal Mrs. Norbey as wielding highly influential power. She might just have been a cagey lady who played up her sweet-old-thing looks. On the other hand, a funny coincidence might in a surprising way prove that Greg and Gene were not entirely wrong about her influence.

In a 2009 interview, Judge B.—who had presided over the legal proceedings regarding the recovery of Greenie—confused the Norbeys with the Maurice Norby family, who actually were prominent in Eau Claire as realtors, assessors, and appraisers. The memory mix-up gives one pause: Did Judge B. make the same mix-up back in the 1970s? That might explain why the judge—as we'll see when the chase gets going—was such a significant roadblock and an inexplicable ally to Mrs. Norbey when legal action to recover Greenie was under way.

Nothing about Mrs. Norbey's history reveals why she took such a stubborn stance regarding Greenie. We know only that she viewed Greg Nelson as disreputable: Perhaps he represented to her the ill appearance of everything new and uncomfortable about Eau Claire. We can only guess at the impact of changing times on Olga and her husband, Leroy. At the time of the fire in 1974 LeRoy was retiring. Change was upon them and we'll never know what it did to them. LeRoy died in 1995 and Olga died two years later. We can't ask them what rubbed them so raw as to set in motion a totally unnecessary crime, a crime that truly could never have resulted in a benefit to them. Perhaps it was spite. Perhaps it was revenge for the betrayals that time had wrought against seniors devoted to the status quo.

It was not until 1976, two years after the fire, that Mrs. Olga Norbey came up against a determined and effective opponent: Gene Brotzman, Greenie's latest advocate.

The Mystery of the Missing Classic

By 2009, the garage behind the house on Vine Street was gone.

Greenie's advocate in disguise.

40

Chapter 4: The Mystery of the Missing Classic

Two years after Greenie's initial capture in 1974 by Mrs. Olga Norbey, a walk up the driveway to the garage behind 508½ Vine Street in Eau Claire—where Greenie is supposed to be held prisoner—ends with a shocking discovery. Greenie is missing! But no one knows that, no one except Mrs. Olga Norbey. In fact, even after nearly three years had elapsed since the car-napping in 1974, all interested parties, including all participating lawyers, still believed that once the lock on the garage door was opened Greenie would be revealed.

So, let's go back to a day two years and 10 months after Greenie's initial capture. On December 3, 1976 Greg Nelson's aunt Dorris, her husband, Gene Brotzman, and their three children visited Greg and Mary Lou at 726 Forest Street, Eau Claire, where the young couple was living in a friend's basement.

It was the first time Dorris and Gene visited with the young couple since their wedding. No one had mentioned a fire or a lost car to Dorris and Gene until that day.

In the course of conversation, Gene asked Greg how the '32 Plymouth Rumble Seat Coupe was running and if he ever took it for rides. Shyly, Greg told the whole sad tale.

"I was dumbfounded to learn what had happened after the fire in 1974," Gene recalls, "and that Mrs. Norbey, incredibly, got away with literally stealing the car from Greg."

The more he learned, the more Gene's hackles rose. He quickly recognized that Greg had simply dropped all attempts to recover Greenie after being told he needed a lawyer. Greg didn't have the money for a lawyer. The whole idea seemed impossible to him and he needed badly to turn his attention to his most pressing financial needs. Gene appreciated Greg's situation—and he also appreciated old, classic cars.

"Do you still have the title to the car?" Gene asked.

"Yes, I do," Greg replied.

Right then and there on that December day when Gene realized that Greg was not able to recover the '32 Plymouth, he offered Greg $2,000 to buy the title. Greg and Mary Lou were more than happy to accept

Chapter 4

In June of the same year that Gene Brotzman purchased the title for Greenie, he was busily tinkering with a Model T Ford. Greenie would pose a challenge to Gene beyond his expectations.

the offer. In 1976, $2,000 was a considerable sum. It was enough to supplement the GI Bill so Greg and Mary Lou could buy a house—the house they lived in right up through their retirement years. Greg would later comment that Gene was the kind of person who liked "to do things others can enjoy."

43

The Stone Wall

Gene wasted no time in pursuing what he saw as plain and simple justice.

"I called Mrs. Norbey on the phone immediately from Greg's apartment and told her I had bought the car from Greg and I demanded immediate possession. She yelled, 'You take back your money. That's my car now.' When I asked her why she was claiming the car was hers, she said Greg caused the fire in her rented apartment. She added further that Greg had also stolen her ladder." At that point Gene turned and asked Greg if he knew where Mrs. Norbey's ladder was. Greg responded that he had loaned it to the neighbor, where it probably still was. Gene turned back to Mrs. Norbey, waiting on the line. "I informed her that the fire department did not blame Greg for the fire. She loudly proclaimed, 'I'll see my lawyer.' I in turn said, 'That is your business. I will definitely be seeing my lawyer.'"

They did both immediately consult their lawyers. Mrs. Norbey must have told her lawyer that Gene said the fire department didn't blame Greg. Together she and her lawyer came up with a new ploy. The next thing Gene knew he was being told a different reason for why Mrs. Norbey claimed to be the owner of the Plymouth. Now the story was that Greg had abandoned the car. It

Chapter 4

was a quick shuffle to a new strategy. The fire was no longer offered as the reason for claiming the car. Now the reason was that two years or so had elapsed before anyone attempted to recover it. Therefore it was abandoned.

Later the story would change again. But the lapse in time between Greg's last attempt at recovery in March 1974 and Gene's first attempt in December 1976 would eventually form the cornerstone of Mrs. Norbey's defense in a pre-trial hearing. At that time—as we'll see in the coming chapters—both Mrs. Norbey's lawyer and the presiding judge expressed the preliminary judgment that Mrs. Norbey had the right to keep the car. Outrageous, don't you think?

But we have a long way to go and a lot of mystery to probe before we see how Gene Brotzman finessed this legal nonsense in advocating for Greenie's return.

Meanwhile, let's face it: our upright citizen, Mrs. Norbey—"the picture of a sweet little old lady" as one lawyer put it—was actually a titan of chutzpah. She not only changed her story and claimed that Greg had abandoned the vehicle but she demanded that $50 a month be paid for the use of the garage on Vine Street. Can you imagine that: at the time of her claim, Greenie had already disappeared from the garage and Mrs. Norbey knew it. So she was capable of stealing the car, causing

45

The Mystery of the Missing Classic

it to vanish, and charging the victim for rental of a garage that was empty.

It took a while for the generous Gene Brotzman, Greenie's only true advocate, to recognize the Big Stone Wall that stood between him and the lovely Plymouth PA Rumble Seat Coupe.

"Wow! Little did I know at the time what I was up against. What a formidable mess I got into when I bought that title."

As soon as he got home to Edgerton, Wisconsin, on December 4, 1976, Gene outlined the problem to John Roethe, his lawyer, and asked him to free up the car so he could take possession of it. And thus the pursuit of justice was put into the hands of lawyers—and the result rivaled *Bleak House*, Charles Dickens' fictional portrayal of lawyers and the legal system.

Roethe didn't want to take a case in Eau Claire since he lived in Edgerton. So he asked attorney H., an associate in Eau Claire, to take Gene's case against Mrs. Norbey. He outlined what he knew of the case. Most of what he said we already know, but for any sleuth joining Gene in unraveling a growing mystery, there were a couple of new tidbits in that letter to H., dated December 8, 1976.

For example, we knew that Greg had no luck when

Chapter 4

he went to the Eau Claire DA in 1974, but H.'s letter adds this piece of information:

"Greg went to the District Attorney in the spring of 1974. The DA called Mrs. Olga Jensen Norbey 'and she was quite vociferous over the telephone.' The DA then called her attorney G. There was no follow-up."

So, Mrs. Chutzpah was not daunted by the DA.

Roethe also expressed the opinion that the car was not abandoned. He asked H. to contact G. In addition, he informed H. that "We anticipate bringing an action for replevin [recovery] of the automobile together with some demand for punitive damages."

In closing his letter Roethe actually confirmed that no one yet knew that Greenie was missing. He told H. that "To clear up any problems, the car is presently located at 508½ Vine St. in Eau Claire."

By December 28, 1976, the record shows H. had taken the case for Gene and had discussed the situation with Mrs. Norbey's lawyer, G. Apparently even G. couldn't get Mrs. Norbey to talk. He tried to call her a number of times and couldn't get her and then wrote a letter to her.

So as 1976 comes to a close, lawyer G. tells lawyer H., who in turn tells Gene the advocate, that they

47

are waiting to hear from Mrs. Norbey. *Waiting* is the operative word here. There will be a lot of that as the chase begins and the mystery of Greenie's imprisonment slowly unfolds.

Lawyers, Lawyers, Lawyers

Over the course of the pursuit to find Greenie, Gene Brotzman grew more than skeptical about the legal profession and began to dot his notes with lawyer jokes. It was the system of billing that finally drove Gene to record the following, hoping it would find its way into this history.

"A lawyer dies and goes to heaven. 'This must be a mistake,' he says to Saint Peter at the Pearly Gates. 'I'm too young to die. I'm only 50.' 'Fifty,' says Saint Peter. 'According to our calculations you're 82.' 'How'd you get that?' the lawyer asks. 'We added up your billable hours.'"

The Mystery of the Missing Classic

Part 2: The Pursuit

The Mystery of the Missing Classic

```
                                EAU CLAIRE, WIS.         November 15, 19 78

   Mr. Gene W. Brotzman              Invoice No. 7906
       c/o Edgerton Community Elementary Schools
          100 Elm High Drive

                    Edgerton, WI 53534


                           IN ACCOUNT WITH

                           ATTORNEYS AT LAW
                              SUITE 201
                       EAU CLAIRE, WISCONSIN 54701


   In Re:  Brotzman -vs- Norbey

   TO:  Services rendered from November 1, 1977 to completion
        (description of services attached) --------------------$975.50

   TO:  Disbursements
           Court reporter for deposition services--$165.25
           Long distance telephone ----------------  13.35
                                                   $178.60
                                                                 178.60

   TOTAL SERVICES AND DISBURSEMENTS -------------------------$1,154.10

                                              NOV 15 PAID
```

An interim bill from Lawyer P., slim evidence of action on his part.

Chapter 5: Hot on the Trail

Leave It to the Lawyers

Actually, only Greenie's advocate Gene Brotzman could be said to be hot in pursuit. Lawyers pursue slowly. Gene set the law in motion on December 4, 1976. At the end of 1976 he and his lawyer John H. were still waiting for Mrs. Norbey's lawyer, G., to get some answers from his evasive and nervy client.

Apparently while they waited, letters flew here and there until Gene grew a touch impatient. "This writing back and forth continued until I had a phone conversation with Olga Norbey's attorney, G.," Gene reported in his growing log of events. The call yielded some new information:

> G. claims that he felt Mrs. Norbey had the green light from Greg Nelson to have the car.

He also quoted Mrs. Norbey as saying she did not know where the car is right now.

So now we have a new story of why the car was seized. It was a gift from Greg Nelson to the worthy Mrs. Norbey, who seems to have misplaced the gift, according to lawyer G. Whatever else this bit of fiction revealed, Greenie's disappearance was now out in the open. But the anxious advocate Gene Brotzman would have to leave the pursuit of justice to the lawyers. How else could he have proceeded? When the law is obviously broken, where could a person go to get justice?

That settled, let's be lawyerly for a while and trace the step-by-step chronology of letters that defined how the lawyers went looking for Greenie.

January 26, 1977—No word yet from Mrs. Norbey. We're still waiting. Only a month or so has elapsed since the wait began. But, at this point Gene still thought he could influence the stately pace of legal actions. So, his log reveals that he took action:

> I felt that my attorney, H., was getting nowhere so I dismissed him and secured the help of attorney P. of [address], Eau Claire.

Unfortunately, the first results from attorney P. won't appear until his letter dated March 10, 1977. In

Chapter 5

the meantime Gene and his terminated lawyer H. exchanged a letter or two.

February 3, 1977—H. to Gene. Lawyer H. acknowledges that he has been replaced, and he offers an explanation of his performance. He and lawyer G. kept trying to get in touch with Mrs. Norbey and finally decided that since she was out of the state, "it would not be economically reasonable to commence an action at this time." He admits that he didn't understand that Gene wanted him to undertake getting Greenie back no matter what. So he charges off his time and apologizes for not returning Gene's call of January 24, claiming the message was misplaced.

February 11, 1977—Gene to G. Antsy once again Gene calls Mrs. Norbey's lawyer G., and gets nothing much for his effort—just a promise that G. will try to get hold of Mrs. Norbey for more facts.

March 10, 1977—P. to Gene. At last we hear from Gene's replacement lawyer, P. P. informs Gene that he has been trying to get in touch with Greg Nelson for an interview and has been unsuccessful to date. P. also reports the following:

> I have had telephone contact with Attorney G. He, in turn, has been in telephone contact with

Mrs. Norbey. Mr. G. states that Mrs. Norbey has informed him that the vehicle is not in the garage anymore, and, in fact has been gone for some time.

G. had no more details, but promised to investigate and provide a full report. In essence, this is all pretty much the same story we heard back in December 1976 when Mrs. Norbey said she "didn't know where the car is." Lawyer G. keeps promising more facts.

April 28, 1977—P. to Gene. Finally, lawyer P. talks to Greg in his office on April 26th, but has nothing to report about the meeting. He tells Gene he wants to check with lawyer G. one more time and if that fails, he will institute a lawsuit asking for the return of the automobile if it's still intact, or for monetary damages. He asks Gene for the value of the auto.

Gene hand wrote the following note at the top of P.'s letter: "suggested value $5,900–$7,000." But it isn't clear that he ever told this to P., who asked for it again in his next letter on July 5.

The Plot Thickens

July 5, 1977—P. to Gene. Note that it is the day after Independence Day when Gene receives new infor-

Chapter 5

mation revealing his dependence on the fictions offered by Mrs. Norbey and lawyer G. You won't believe what lawyer P. reported that day:

> I met with Attorney G. on June 30. According to him, the automobile was hauled away by the junk man from a neighboring small community quite some time ago. According to him, Mrs. Norbey did not receive any money for this, and she is not sure who the junk man is. Mr. G. states that his firm has attempted to track down the junk man, but has not been able to do so. Therefore, the whereabouts of the car remain a mystery.

There you have it, the legal opinion after six months of investigation. It's a mystery. The junk man took it. But, to be fair, lawyer P. did not let the case rest.

He asked Gene if he wanted to pursue a settlement, because he thought lawyer G. had hinted at that possibility. "If not," P. proposed, "the only two alternatives left are to continue the search for the junk man or start legal proceedings."

It seems Gene didn't buy the idea of hunting down an anonymous junk man. His log of events notes that he and the lawyers P. and G. exchanged letters and phone calls following the July 5 revelation about the

The Mystery of the Missing Classic

junk man. The upshot of all that buzz was the notice that follows.

> **August 1, 1977**—P. to Gene.
> RE: Gene W. Brotzman vs. Olga J. Norbey.
>
> I have filed a Summons and Complaint starting an action on your behalf against Mrs. Norbey. The Summons and Complaint were served on her on July 22. I will let you know as soon as her attorney(s) have responded.

At last, action! But don't hold your breath waiting for the case to speed along. The next recorded contact between Gene and any lawyer came almost three months later.

October 24, 1977—Gene to P. After thanking lawyer P. for the August 1st notice, Gene asks for an update and expresses concern about obstacles to getting Mrs. Norbey's deposition, to expedite legal proceedings.

> It has been 3 months since I last heard from you and I am wondering if you would update me on the progress of the action. I assume Mrs. Norbey will be heading south for the winter

soon. Hopefully this will not have to be postponed until spring.

It is my understanding that you would have included punitive damages in the summons and complaint.

You would think that things should get moving now toward an actual court date, a final hearing. But, nope. First there has to be a date set for a conference with a judge to set up a schedule of dates for the various stages of the crossed and bossed proceedings. But take comfort, there is no mention of having to first settle the shape of the conference table!

November 2, 1977—P. to Gene. Lawyer P. was obviously inspired by Gene's October 24th letter. By November 2, he had speedily contacted Judge B., who set a scheduling conference for November 17 to settle on deadlines for motions and discovery proceedings.

As a further demonstration of his confidence in taken bold action, lawyer P. enclosed his interim bill.

Following this letter we have a pause for more waiting—a good time to celebrate the first anniversary of Gene Brotzman vs. Olga Norbey.

December 28, 1977—P. to Gene. The scheduling

conference was held before Judge B. on November 17 and lawyer P. apologizes to Gene for not writing sooner. He was busy trying to depose Mrs. Norbey.

> This was complicated by the fact she has gone to Florida for the winter. I attempted to determine whether there was a time she was coming back to Wisconsin over the holidays. Apparently she is not coming back for that purpose, so it will be necessary for her to fly back for the purpose of depositions.
>
> I have suggested to Attorney G. that we depose Mrs. Norbey on Monday, January 16. He may also be interested in taking your deposition, and possibly that of Greg Nelson.

Welcome to 1978

So lawyer P. proposed the deposition thing be held on January 16. Ha! Who believes that Mrs. Norbey, the queen of chutzpah, is going to get on a plane especially to fly back to Wisconsin and spill the beans about Greenie? Forget about it!

February 16, 1978—P. to Gene. Norbey can't come. She's in the hospital down there in sunny Florida. Lawyer P. confesses to having attended a pretrial conference on February 13. At that conference lawyer G. announced he had just discovered Mrs. Norbey's state of health. She has become ill and has been hospitalized. It is not possible to schedule depositions. G. expects her in April and will schedule depositions for all at that time.

Between February 21, 1978 and March 1st, Gene and lawyer P. discussed the need to meet and articulate a plan. They set the date for a strategy conference on March 11. Lawyer P., during the exchange of letters, took the opportunity to announce his new address in the law firm B., W., and P.

No one left notes about what happened at the conference between Gene and lawyer P., but we can infer from the next recorded letter that skepticism arose over the new Norbey delaying tactic—her tale of illness and hospitals.

March 13, 1978—P. to G. Lawyer P. informed lawyer G. that he had met with Gene Brotzman, who traveled the three hours from his home in Edgerton to Eau Claire for the meeting.

> Mr. Brotzman is anxious to move things along. Furthermore, because of his prior experience with Mrs. Norbey, he is naturally suspicious

The Mystery of the Missing Classic

about the validity of her claim that she is not able to return to Eau Claire for depositions due to her hospitalization.

Would you please ask Mrs. Norbey to provide a doctor's statement verifying her present inability to return to Eau Claire, and predicting when she will be able to return.

March 13, 1978—Gene to himself. On the back of lawyer P.'s letter, Gene scribbled notes that sound like he talked to Mrs. Norbey. She apparently said she saw the car in the garage at the end of August back in 1974. She had her husband take it out of the garage and put it along the side of the garage by the alley. They needed room. In the early part of September the car was gone. She then mentioned that a carpenter working on the fire-damaged apartment saw the car and liked it. She thought the car was an old junker, not an antique.

This is shocking news. Unfortunately Gene's scribbled note is the only place these comments are acknowledged and the note is not dated. So whenever the confession took place, Mrs. Norbey did at some point confess to Gene that the car has been missing since September of 1974!

Chapter 5

March 17, 1978—P. to Gene. Lawyer P. reports receiving a letter from lawyer G. saying he received an unsolicited letter from Mrs. Norbey. She is still in Florida and has been hospitalized three times during the months of January and February. She expects to return to Eau Claire in April if she can travel by car. Lawyer G. thinks that in response to Gene's request for doctor verification, Mrs. Norbey's letter is "sufficient substantiation."

Lawyer P. advises Gene that he can't force the issue because the judge permitted them until May 15 to complete the depositions. If she doesn't return in time, the judge can force her to provide verification of her hospitalization.

This is the first we have learned that the important scheduling conference with Judge B. back in November 1977 resulted in delaying depositions to a deadline of May 15, 1978. Sometimes the stately march of the law takes your breath away. Imagine Gene's reaction to this latest obfuscation. His reaction actually turns up five days after lawyer P.'s letter in a long, hand-written list of points that Gene wanted to make to P. Apparently Gene was not simply and idly waiting for the lawyers.

March 22, 1978—Gene's handwritten notes on points to make to P. In his notes, Gene says he reported

The Mystery of the Missing Classic

the situation to Chief Wall of the local Edgerton police department. Chief Wall called the local district attorney who said it seemed as though Gene's attorney was "not on the ball." He felt this matter should have had a court appearance long before this time and raised questions about P.'s ability to handle the case.

Gene then called the Eau Claire police who thought it was more a title dispute, a civil suit rather than a stolen car case. Both Chief Wall and the Edgerton DA urged Gene to take his case to Eau Claire and file a complaint for replevin now. They both felt that lawyer G. would not have advised Norbey to sell the car. They also agreed with Gene that she wouldn't give a $7,000 car to a junk dealer.

At this point in his notes Gene speculates about the influence behind the delays—"some indications had come out of Eau Claire that G. is a powerful attorney who other attorneys are afraid to stand up to."

Gene ends his note clearly convinced that "G. knows where the car is along with Norbey." He decides that if there is no deposition by May 1, he will assume they are stalling and will take the *Milwaukee Journal* investigative reporting route.

These forceful assertions were reported to lawyer P. over the phone. But Gene did not go to the *Milwaukee Journal*, as May 1, 1978 passed him by.

Chapter 5

May 16, 1978—P. to Gene. Lawyer P. reports that the second pre-trial conference was held on May 15. At that time lawyer G. told those assembled that Mrs. Norbey had returned two weeks ago. But a major fire at a lumber company next door kept her busy with damages to her house.

Just in case Gene might be a bit reluctant to swallow the fire story, P. vouched for it—that major fire "was indeed a major fire."

But the good news is something actually happened. The lawyers P. and G. scheduled a deposition for Friday, June 9, where G. wants to depose Gene and probably Greg Nelson. P. will depose Mrs. Norbey. Gene agrees. A deposition day means they'll all be together swearing to the truth of the matter.

Terrific! After a year and a half, the valiant advocate has the wily Mrs. Norbey backed up to the edge of the precipice. Will she escape like an old-time movie serial villain, maybe hanging off the edge of the courthouse third floor windowsill to be picked up by Mr. Norbey in his trusty cheatmobile? Or will she simply tell tales under oath?

The Mystery of the Missing Classic

Gene took detailed notes at the deposition, and followed up with a letter to his lawyer a few days later.

Chapter 6: The Scene of the Real Crime

Fictions delivered outside the legal system are nothing more than stories told. No legal decision is necessary and no legal punishments called for. A deposition, on the other hand, is a sworn statement and has legal weight. You can tell stories all night long out in the civilian world, but once you swear to them in a deposition, you'd better not be lying.

Just for fun let's recap the fictions Mrs. Norbey offered in the months that led up to the June 9, 1978 day of depositions:

- Greenie is compensation for fire damage.
- Greenie was abandoned by Greg Nelson and therefore is the legal property of the landlady, Mrs. Norbey.
- Greenie was off-handedly given to Mrs. Norbey by Greg Nelson.

- Greenie was taken from the alleyway next to Greg's old apartment by a junk man.

Contradictions or not, there's no crime here. But hold your breath, the day of reckoning is upon us…we hope!

June 9, 1978—The Day of Depositions

We're sitting at a large table in lawyer G.'s office—home turf, you might say, for Mrs. Norbey, "the picture of a sweet little old lady." Lawyer P. sits at one end of the table, flanked by Greg Nelson and the advocate/plaintiff, Gene Brotzman. Sitting on the other far end of the table is a tape recorder, placed by lawyer G. There is a pause while the visiting three await the grand entrance.

Enter lawyer G., walking slowly, lending his arm to Mrs. Norbey who leans on him just slightly enough to make her limp obvious. G. seats her opposite where he intends to sit. He eases her into her chair and thoughtfully places a footstool beneath her left leg. "Are you comfortable?" he asks before seating himself.

Introductions are conducted, and Mrs. Norbey makes her first comment aimed directly at Gene, "If I had known you were such a nice man, I'd have handled this differently."

Chew on that for a while! On what basis did Olga

Chapter 6

Norbey determine—after her elaborate seating ritual—that Gene was a nice man? Of course, Gene does happen to be a good guy...and he isn't scruffy. But what about those angry phone calls in their history? Has she written them off a mere minute or two after catching her first sight of Gene? Are we witnessing flattery, witchery, strategy, or the clueless offering of a sweet little old lady?

Lawyer P. begins questioning Mrs. Norbey. As the questioning goes on, Mrs. Norbey looks to her lawyer G. before answering. G. frequently interrupts P. to tell his client, "Just answer 'no' if you don't know." The tale evoked by P.'s questioning boils down to the following narrative taken from Gene Brotzman's notes and delivered with a bit of poetic license in Mrs. Norbey's voice:

> When I got back from Florida on the 14th or 15th of April 1974, I saw the car in the garage. And there was furniture still in the Nelson's burned-out apartment. I was there to meet with the fire inspector the day after the fire.

Wait a second. How could she come home on April 14th or 15th and meet with the fire inspector the day after the fire—which happened on March 24th as lawyer G. established in his deposing of Greg Nelson?

67

The Mystery of the Missing Classic

Was this a senior moment for Mrs. Norbey? Or does she have time travel talent? She continues under questioning.

> Around April 25th I saw the car still in the garage when the carpenters were there. One of the carpenters was interested in buying the car. I didn't see the car again until the end of August or in September. I had my husband take the car out of the garage, hoping that the young man [Greg] would come and get it. I needed room in that garage. I had my husband put the car beside the garage near the alley. I saw the car there several times.
>
> In the early part of September I saw the car was gone. I don't know what happened to it. I didn't ask anyone to take it. A junk man asked about the car after it was sitting outside the garage for about a week. I don't know who he was. The workmen working on the apartment were still there. One of the workmen asked whose car it was. I told him it belonged to a former tenant. The car had a cracked windshield. It was just an old, junky car.

Under further questioning by lawyer P., Mrs. Norbey noted that some man from the Eau Claire District

Chapter 6

Attorney's office had contacted her in July and later in August. The DA told her that Greg had visited his office and not paid for his visit. (Why would Greg be expected to pay to consult a public official?) The DA said when Greg did not call for the car, he had abandoned it and Olga could dispose of it. He didn't think Greg looked like a reputable character.

After some factual questioning of Greg Nelson by lawyer G. concerning the exact description of the car, license, insurance, and other such niggling time-wasters, the deposition day concluded. Mrs. Norbey repeated her first comment of the day about doing it differently if she had known Gene was such a nice guy. Lawyer G. informed every one that

> [T]he tape of the depositions will go to Judge B. Judge B. will decide whether there is sufficient data to warrant a jury trial, or whether it is clear what direction a decision should go and for what reasons.

Does it seem fair to you that this vital event should be run by the defendant's lawyer with no neutral third party present? Greenie's advocate, Gene Brotzman had his doubts.

The Mystery of the Missing Classic

The Brotzman Interpretation

To begin with, Mrs. Norbey's twice-made "nice man" comment raised Gene's suspicions. He notes this in a letter to lawyer P. on June 19, 1978. Norbey's comment leads Gene to conclude she was out to get Greg Nelson because he seemed like a "disreputable character."

Time out from Gene's Interpretation: This might be a good time to take note of Mrs. Norbey's rental policies. She didn't use written leases and gave no receipts. Her brother or sister-in-law collected the rent. So she only really saw Greg Nelson around the time of the fire. Her rental policies seemed as if they were designed for transients who make month-by-month arrangements. It's possible she held a low opinion of all her tenants. Given her policies and the poorly heated and cobbled-together state of the property, if she had been operating in New York or Chicago rather than Eau Claire, you might say she was a slumlord.

Gene's interpretation never implies such a thing, but he does suspect her new story about the workman, or carpenter as Gene calls him in his letter to lawyer P.:

> Mrs. Norbey's comment about one of the carpenter's interest in the '32 Plymouth coupe leads me, and I'm sure you, to believe a few questions should be asked of them. It could

Chapter 6

well be Mrs. Norbey sold the car to one of the carpenters.

Could that be? Could she sell the car without having possession of the title? Apparently that didn't occur to Gene, or perhaps he felt her capable of forging a title. In any case, he simply goes on to tell lawyer P. why he thinks lawyer G. insisted on sitting across from Mrs. Norbey.

> During your deposition of Mrs. Norbey, and while you were writing, Mr. G. constantly gave Mrs. Norbey nods and head shakes, as to what to say or not to say. Before she would give answers to any question, she'd glance at Mr. G. who would give almost unnoticeable head movements such as up and down for "answer yes" or sideways for "answer no." Mr. G. would frequently interrupt your questioning and say to Mrs. Norbey: "Just answer no if you don't know." That was telling her to answer "no." This is of course why he wanted her directly across from him at the large table during your deposition.

Gene may be on to something here. Remember, Judge B., who will be deciding the case, will only

71

hear the tape. He won't see any of the coaching that Gene observed. Of course, the judge also won't see the Norbey/G. grand entrance with footstool and all. But, then Gene noted that after lawyer P. asked his first question of Mrs. Norbey, she leaned forward, removed her foot from the foot stool, and never put it back.

The Saving Mistake

Does it feel like the deck is stacked against Greenie and her advocate? Gene's interpretation of the deposition reveals just a tiny touch of the beleaguered man's defensiveness.

On the other hand, there was no way at this point that Gene would recognize Mrs. Norbey's truly big mistake. As events unfurl in the coming few months, we will discover that she lied under oath during this deposition. That could give Gene some leverage over her.

But, first Judge B. has to review the depositions and give his opinion. And in the face of that opinion—which you will read about in the next chapter—Gene might be justified in suspecting what looks like a bit of collusion between the judge and Mrs. Norbey's lawyer G. Or if it's not collusion, it sure makes the legal system smell bad. We shall see what we shall see!

Chapter 7: A Race Against Time

The Judge's Prognosis

Seven weeks after the depositions were taken, Gene heard from lawyer P. And the news was not good. P. had other obligations on the day of the pre-trial conference so another lawyer from his agency—Lawyer W.—attended the conference with Judge B. and lawyer G. representing Mrs. Norbey.

Keep in mind what Judge B. heard from the depositions—probably something like this: A disreputable young man left his old car sitting in poor, dear Mrs. Norbey's garage until she was forced to put it outside. And soon it was gone. Then, after two years or so, the scruffy young man's uncle wants the car.

In examining the evidence, apparently no one asked how the person who took the car got it started. Who

The Mystery of the Missing Classic

The activities of the legal professionals in this case would be comical, if fair play were not at stake.

Chapter 7

had the keys? No one asked how Mrs. Norbey could claim ownership without a title. No one even pointed out the inconsistencies in her deposition, particularly her claim that she met with the fire chief the day after the fire, even though she didn't get into town until a few weeks later.

Nonetheless, Judge B. had a strong opinion about all this, which was rendered at the July 31, 1978 pre-trial conference and relayed to Gene by lawyer P. in a letter dated August 1. Gene recorded P.'s letter in his log of events, and stewed over the disturbing language P. used.

> Judge B. strongly inferred that he has serious doubts about the strength of our case. Although he recognized that Greg did try a few times to recover the car shortly after the fire in March of 1974, the judge was dismayed by the long period of time during which nothing was done, namely until you purchased title to the car on December 4, 1974.
>
> I gather that it is his opinion that this long delay will be fatal to the case. As a result, he again strongly inferred that we would be better off settling the case for a nominal consideration rather than pursuing a trial.

The Mystery of the Missing Classic

Wait a minute. We have to stop and notice the remarkable legal language here. This judge, who really doesn't know the value of the car or even the real facts of the case, is dismayed by the lapse in time, which leads him to strongly infer that Gene settle for a nominal consideration. Knowing what we now know, don't you find that just a little dismaying? Well, listen to this next bit of information from lawyer P. to Gene.

> In many respects a judge exercises life and death control over a lawsuit. In your case we have requested a jury trial. However, even with a jury, the judge can, if he believes the evidence merits, take the case away from the jury and decide it himself. This is done when the judge believes the evidence can only lead to one conclusion. I doubt that the judge would do that here, although it is a possibility.
>
> Even more troublesome, after a jury has reached its decision, the losing party can present a motion asking the judge to set aside the jury verdict and determine that they should have been the winners. Furthermore, even during the course of the trial, a judge can make matters extremely difficult for one side if he believes that their case has little or no merit.

Chapter 7

Considering the judge's view of this case, I would fully expect that he will make the trial extremely difficult and I would predict that if the jury should decide in your favor, the judge is likely to set aside the jury verdict and grant judgment to Mrs. Norbey.

In other words, the judge has Gene by the carburetor and Gene ain't going nowhere. What's more, his lawyer is ready to crumble like some week-old piece of cake. In fact, from the beginning of his letter to the end lawyer P. loses more and more confidence. He starts out saying he doubted the judge would use his power to set aside the jury decision in Gene's case, although it's possible... and by the end of the letter it is a likelihood that Judge B. will set the verdict aside and grant judgment to Mrs. Norbey. If this letter is a model of lawyer P.'s backbone, should he get to court he might start out the court trial pleading Gene's case and end up telling the jury to just give the car to Mrs. Norbey because the judge will anyway. Lawyer P.'s letter continued:

> We should evaluate the case to see whether a jury would be likely to rule in your favor. This is difficult to predict, because your case comes down to a simple question of credibility, namely, whom is the jury going to believe. It

77

> is further complicated by the fact that we have what is called the burden of proof. This means that it is our job to convince the jury that our evidence when weighed against the opposing evidence has more convincing power. If the jury is not convinced either way, it must decide against you.
>
> Once again, it is the judge's opinion, even though we may disagree, that we cannot meet the burden of proof. All of this is extremely distressing. However, I have always believed that I should keep my clients fully informed of the bad news as well as the good news.

No wonder Gene began to suspect collusion between the two lawyers and the judge based on lawyer G.'s influence on behalf of his sweet little old client, Mrs. Norbey. Perhaps lawyer P. is a touch afraid to come up against the powerful lawyer G. Here's the best lawyer P. can do for Gene:

> My job is to offer you the best legal advice I can. Under these circumstances, I am left with no alternative but to recommend that you consider a settlement of your claim against Mrs. Norbey.

Chapter 7

Gene's response to all this does not mince words. He was

> struck dumbfounded as well as totally devastated. To me, and as a result of Mr. G. and Mrs. Norbey's actions at the depositions, it was obvious that both of them were hiding something. Some facts... are known only by them.

To pour salt in Gene's wounds, lawyer P. sends another letter on August 23, 1978 saying that the settlement he asked for is $3,000. However, the most Mrs. Norbey will settle for is $500. That was the amount Judge B. had recommended. Lawyer P. goes on to give some details on how their case has fallen apart and concludes:

> I am extremely concerned about the dim outlook for your case. It is my sincere opinion that any money you spend from now on will in all probability be money down the drain.

Gene might well have said that it's all been money down the drain. In fact, he kind of implies this in his recorded response:

> By this time I was getting to the end of my patience and could not contain my furious

thoughts at the nearly two years of inactivity and lack of progress on retrieval of the '32 Plymouth.

But this outrage grows even more painful to contemplate when we learn what Gene was going through in his daily life.

This Is Almost Too Sad for Words

In the midst of the news about the outrageous miscarriage of justice, Gene had to face one of life's most devastating realities. On the same day he recorded Judge B.'s opinion, he also recorded this plaintive entry:

> My wife, Dorris I. Nelson Brotzman, a first grade teacher at Milton, Wisconsin Elementary School, was coming to the end of a two-year struggle with breast cancer. She knew her life was ebbing. She voiced her hope to see the '32 Plymouth Coupe returned to its rightful owner before leaving this earthly scene.
>
> She continued teaching at Milton to the end of the 1977–78 school year. Less than three months later, on August 12, 1978 she passed away at the age of 46. My grief was so heavy that I had great difficulty keeping focused on the problem at hand.

Chapter 7

Can you imagine the difficulty, facing death and injustice within a few days of each other? Then imagine carrying on with the responsibilities of a school principal to a huge teaching staff and student population, as Gene did. "All seemed to be caving in on me," he noted with characteristic restraint.

Recovery of Greenie now took on an added importance for Gene. He had shared the tales of his attempt at justice with his wife whom he lost at the lowest moment of his hopes. Even in her last days she continued to wish to see Greenie come home. Now Gene needed to fulfill their shared aspiration. In a later newspaper article Gene said he loved that old car but a large part of his love came from his wife's affection for it. "I had to get it back because I knew how much she wanted it," he said.

A Deadline and a Challenge to the Grieving Advocate

After urging "the plaintiff to consider carefully his evidence in relationship to the legal theories upon which the action is founded," Judge B. throws down the challenge to Gene's grief-stricken heart: A trial before a six-person jury, estimated to take one and one-half days, shall begin at 9:00 a.m. Tuesday, November 7, 1978.

Chapter 7 — The Mystery of the Missing Classic

It took until September 6, 1978 for Gene to respond:

> It was at this time that I had gotten the school staff oriented, schedules made, and school started. That included also completion of my dear wife's affairs after her death on August 12th and funeral on the 15th.
>
> I called attorney P. to stop everything, the letter writing, the conferencing, the phone calls, etc. I had resolved that the only way that justice could be reached and Mrs. Norbey forced to give up a possession I believed she had which was legally mine was to go to the Eau Claire newspaper and use publicity of the case to put pressure where it must be in order to reach a fair conclusion.

What an irony. The court date Gene sought for almost two years is now a deadline, November 7, 1978, the day he fears he will lose the car for good.

Cast alone on a sea of questionable conduct, grieving for his lost spouse, all hopes of recovering Greenie blasted by an ill-informed judge in a twisted legal system, Gene could well have looked to the sky and called out: This is a job for Superman.

But instead he looked to the power of the press and,

Chapter 7

```
STATE OF WISCONSIN        CIRCUIT COURT        EAU CLAIRE COUNTY
* * * * * * * * * * * * * * * * * * * * * * * * * * * * * * *
                                **
GENE W. BROTZMAN,
                                **
                PLAINTIFF,
                                **    ORDER RESULTING FROM
      vs.                       **    PRETRIAL CONFERENCE
                                **    CASE NO. 77CV273
OLGA J. NORBEY,
                                **
                DEFENDANT.
                                **
* * * * * * * * * * * * * * * * * * * * * * * * * * * * * * *
      A pretrial conference was held July 31, 1978.  Appearing were
```

Order Resulting From Pretrial Conference Case No. 77CV273 regarding Gene W. Brotzman, Plaintiff, vs Olga J. Norbey, Defendant.

in a manner of speaking, called for the aid of Clark Kent, newspaperman, to help find the car before November 7 when it will be lost to injustice. A shrewd move, don't you think? Or whistling up an empty alley?

83

Chapter 8: Voluntary Clues

Outrage Leads to Action

On top of recognizing that the court date of November 7, 1978 was a threat to his hopes rather than a promise of justice, Gene also saw the enormity of his position with the lawyers. He owed P. more than $2,000, and as he notes in his log of events:

> Judge B. and attorney G. were suggesting that I drop the case, accept $500 from Mrs. Norbey to "get off her back" so to speak!!
>
> Then I would have all the bills to pay! Not on my life would I accept such ridiculous terms when I was sure that there was a better solution to this case.

Gene was upset. Just take note of the double excla-

The Mystery of the Missing Classic

> **$500 REWARD**
>
> **$500 REWARD**
>
> $500 REWARD for information leading to the return of this car to its owner. This 1932 Plymouth Coupe with rumble seat was light green with black fenders. It was allegedly stolen from near Mrs. Leroy Norbey's garage at one of her rental homes on 508½ Vine St., Eau Claire. The car had been stored in Mrs. Norbey's garage in the alley at 508½ Vine St. until it was placed outside of the garage about the first week in September of 1974. Efforts have been made to locate the car for returning it to its owner, Gene W. Brotzman of 483 Washington Road, Edgerton, Wisconsin. The car's Identification Number is PB23455. It may have been repainted.
>
> If you have any infomation on this car call collect at 608-884-6007 or 608-884-3381.

Gene placed an ad in the Eau Claire Leader Telegram *offering a reward for information leading to the return of Greenie to her rightful owner.*

mation points in the quote above if you want to know just how deep the upset went. Whenever you see an educator use two exclamation points—a clear violation of the stylistic norm recommended by all the best gram-

Chapter 8

marians—then you know the educator has exploded over the edge of emphasis!!

Within a few frustrated breaths of telling P. to hold his horses, Gene seized the moment and submitted a photo of the car with a short ad to the *Eau Claire Leader-Telegram*:

> $500 REWARD for information leading to the return of this car to its owner. This 1932 Plymouth Coupe with rumble seat was light green with black fenders. It was allegedly stolen from near Mrs. Gordon Norbey's garage at one of her rental homes on 508½ Vine Street, Eau Claire. The car had been stored in Mrs. Norbey's garage in the alley of 508½ Vine Street until it was placed outside of the garage about the first week in September of 1974. Efforts have been made to locate the car for returning it to its owner Gene W. Brotzman of 483 Washington Road, Edgerton, Wisconsin. The car's Identification Number is PB23455. It may have been repainted. If you have any information on this car, call collect at 608-884-6007 or 608-884-3381.

Unfortunately, there were two mistakes made with the first run of this ad. The paper didn't follow direc-

The Mystery of the Missing Classic

tions and instead of printing a 6" by 6" ad (3 columns wide), the paper printed it as a 2" by 3" ad. That's too tiny to notice and it drew no responses.

The second mistake was Gene's: Mrs. Norbey was not Mrs. Gordon Norbey as the ad said, but was Mrs. LeRoy Norbey. Both mistakes were corrected after Gene sent in specific instructions.

Most newspapers do a "make good" to atone for a mistake like the one the *Leader-Telegram* made. But this time the newspaper did more than a free printing. It also printed a fair-sized article along with the ad on Tuesday, September 26, 1978. It told the basic story of Gene Brotzman and Olga Norbey. It quoted lawyer P. as saying the case "stretches the imagination." P. also added his usual both sides of the aisle comments:

> We have a lot stronger case if we find the car. There may be a question about whether or not we have enough evidence to go through with a trial. Finding the car could exonerate Mrs. Norby [sic]. Maybe we could locate the car and find that somebody stole it, and we wouldn't have a case against Mrs. Norby [sic].

Gene might not have thought exonerating Mrs. Norbey was worth mentioning. In any case, this article was a help to Gene's search, but we should note that

Chapter 8

the article spelled Mrs. Norbey wrong—it called her Mrs. Norby. It was clearly the paper's fault, not P.'s. But it raises a curious question. There was actually a Mrs. Norby in Eau Claire at the time of the case in 1978. She was a woman of notable local power. Our Mrs. Norbey was a landlady owning several properties, but no powerhouse.

Here's the kicker to this little observation: the important Judge B. in a written response to questions for this book in 2009 remembered a Mrs. Norby as the defendant. Could he have possibly mixed the two up at the time of the case back in 1978? Did he think he was dealing with the powerful Mrs. Norby? Go ahead, put that speculation in your paranoia pipe—and see if you might be able to puff out some extra sympathy for Gene's suspicion that there were powers exercised behind the scenes.

On Friday, September 29, three days after the *Eau Claire Leader-Telegram* article appeared, *The Post-Crescent*, Appleton-Neenah-Menasha, Wisconsin, printed a brief version of the same article, still spelling Mrs. Norbey wrong but offering a few new words from lawyer P.

P. said he had never heard of advertising being used in such a situation. It was Gene Brotzman's idea. P. chuckled when he added that it seems to be working in

The Mystery of the Missing Classic

this case.... "We've gotten some responses; none that I can discuss, of course."

Chuckle away, lawyer P., the best is yet to come.

Putting Together the Pieces of the Puzzle

Phone calls and letters started coming in only four days after the corrected ad appeared. The willingness of people to respond to Gene's ad is impressive—of course, the $500 reward was probably a bit of a tickler to good citizenship. The leads poured in on October 3 and 4. Here are a few of the most relevant clues.

CLUE NUMBER 1:

A note from Mrs. Homer (Joyce) Borum, of Eau Claire told Gene,

> I am quite sure I saw this car or one very like it in a homecoming parade at Barron, Wisconsin, the first part of July, '78. Perhaps the sheriff there could track this through their local parade committee or someone there may recall the car and occupants. Good luck!

CLUE NUMBER 2:

A phone call from a neighbor offered more than a clue. It offered evidence. The caller lived down the street from the place that caught fire—the place Greg

Chapter 8

and Mary Lou rented from Mrs. Norbey—508½ Vine Street, Eau Claire.

The nameless caller from the neighborhood told Gene that he regularly walked his dog up the alley past the garage where the old car was stored. He knew the place well and he could vouch for the fact that the car never did sit outside the garage. What's more, one day he and his dog walked past a pickup and trailer loading the old Coupe from the garage. He couldn't describe any of the people involved, but he would be willing to testify in court.

"Bingo! I had my first proof that Mrs. Norbey lied under oath!!" Gene noted in his log with jubilation (and double exclamation points). Greenie was still missing, but the nameless neighbor confirmed the crime.

CLUE NUMBER 3:

Paul Heebink, a 27-year old real estate agent in Eau Claire, was out riding some time in the summer of 1977 when he spotted a house for sale on the corner of Bellview and Holm streets. The sign said "For sale by owner. Inquire within." So Paul knocked on the door, hoping to get the house as his listing. A man named G.G. answered. G.G. was sellng his mother and father's house for them. After a little chat, Paul realized it was no dice for getting the listing.

The Mystery of the Missing Classic

But, here is where Fate starts putting in its thumb and coming up with a plum. This Mr. Heebink just happened to notice an old car in the G.G. garage covered with a tarp. He asked to see the car—and wouldn't you know it, up went the tarp and there stood an old Coupe, light-green with black fenders and yellow wheels. Heebink asked if it was for sale. Mr. G.G. said it was his aunt's car and it was tied up in an estate.

The phone call from Heebink relaying his encounter with G.G. excited Gene's advocate instincts. He leapt on the lead. He arranged a time to meet with Paul Heebink and visit the house where the car was spotted. On the day of the appointment, Gene also had time to look into Clue Number 4.

CLUE NUMBER 4:

A "lady" had called lawyer P. and told him that about a year earlier a man named James Jacobson, who lives "towards Fall Creek from Eau Claire," was trying to sell her husband a car similar to Greenie. Her husband buys old cars. This was worth a follow-up and Jacobson's place was not far from Heebink's house. So Gene set off on the trail of Clues 3 and 4.

On the way to Eau Claire, Gene stopped in Durand and spent an overnight visit with his mom. He and she talked over the car situation. They recalled Gene's wife

Chapter 8

Dorris and her desire to see Greenie before she died. Gene drew considerable comfort from the talk. He noted that he got his first good night's sleep in awhile.

The next day, while waiting to meet with Mr. Heebink and visit the house where Heebink saw the car that could be Greenie, Gene set out to follow up on Clue Number 4. He found James Jacobson, a man he described as stocky with large biceps and a friendly smile. "He had the appearance of a hard-working mechanic," Gene thought.

As it turned out, Jacobson knew nothing of a '32 Plymouth but he was proud to show off his restored '31 Ford pickup. Gene took time to enjoy the purr of the Ford's engine. He got to see several more cars in the process of restoration and took a shine to a 1957 Studebaker that was in good original condition and didn't need much restoration. Gene bought it for $200.

Now this may seem like a slackening of Gene's obsessive search. But the purchase was just a little sidetrack—an offering from Gene, let's say, to the wondrous Fate that brought him Paul Heebink and Clue Number 3.

Fate Leads Gene Down a Thorny Path

Of course Fate enjoys toying with its subjects and for that reason is said to be a fickle friend. Fate would,

The Mystery of the Missing Classic

for example, point Gene toward the house where Paul Heebink thought he saw Greenie, but the house will be sold by the time Gene and Paul get there. Ho! Ho! Ho!

And yet anybody chosen to be favored by Fate should be able to manage these little disappointments. Not satisfied with leaving things at a dead end, Gene questioned the new owner. Yes, there had been a 1932 Plymouth Coupe covered up in the garage when the new owner moved in. The new owner had asked the old owner, G.G., if the car was for sale and got the same answer we've already heard. The car belongs to G.G.'s aunt and is tied up in an estate.

Under Gene's further casual questioning, the new owner guessed that the person who came to pick up the car was G.G.'s brother-in-law, and he further guessed that the brother-in-law worked for Brumberg Oil Company.

A new search ensued. There was no Brumberg Oil Company in Eau Claire, but after questioning a few gas station attendants, Gene and Paul discovered Brumberg Oil Company was in Altoona, just three miles from Eau Claire. Off they went to Altoona.

Aw shucks, Brumberg Oil Company was closed when they got there. Gene called the company just on a hunch. He reached a friendly company operator, and asked her the unlikely question of whether someone

Chapter 8

who worked there was a brother-in-law of a G.G. The operator had never even heard of G.G., let alone any brother-in-law, but she promised to make inquiries.

Imagine someone calling you up and saying: "There's this guy you don't know, can you tell me where I can find his brother-in-law?" Greenie's advocate Gene Brotzman has got to be a charmer to pull this one off. The operator, working after hours at Brumberg Oil, agreed that Gene would give her a little time and then call back to see what she had discovered.

Gene then took Paul Heebink back home where his girlfriend and parents were all visiting. Next Gene went to a Perkin's Cake and Steak Restaurant, had a little refreshment, and hoped his leads would not peter out. The Fates must have taken note of his caloried and fortified regeneration. The winds of uncertainty were about to come blowing his way again.

Gene got back on the phone to Brumberg and reached the helpful operator. She could offer little help. No one had heard of G.G. There was one employee, Don Raymond, out on vacation who might know something, the operator kindly remarked. A feeble clue at best—does it sound like it offers a chance in a million of leading to anything? It apparently sounded promising to Greenie's advocate. Gene pressed on, ready to grab hold of the tiniest thread of possibility and swing into

95

The Mystery of the Missing Classic

action. He called Don Raymond, got no answer, but—yielding no ground to Fate's funny turns—he went to Mr. Raymond's house anyway. Fate loves the persistent.

Gene got there in the nick of time, as Mr. and Mrs. Raymond were headed down their driveway to their packed-up car. Oddly enough, Don Raymond knew who G.G. was but hadn't seen him for many years. Don also knew G.G.'s sister and offered to lead Gene to the sister's house since he and his family were headed out that very moment and would pass by the house.

Once again, it looks like Fate was having fun with Gene. This Don Raymond—who is really just a random employee of an oil company that had nothing to do with G.G.—by chance knows G.G. and his sister from the old days. Is this an uncanny coincidence? Yes, but Fate still has a few more corners for Gene to turn.

After a little confusion and a drive through the small town of Hatley, east of Eau Claire, Don Raymond and his family finally led Gene to the house of Glenn Hoover, who actually worked for a local Standard Oil company, not Brumberg Oil.

Hoover confessed to being G.G.'s brother-in-law, but denied storing or hauling any '32 Plymouth Coupe. Oops, another dead end? This guy, Glenn, was really emphatic. No car, period. Gene "dismissed" himself and went to Paul Heebink's house to think about it.

Chapter 8

No More Cosmic Jokes

Gene still suspected that G.G. was the key to the mystery of Greenie's disappearance. Heebink, besides being a gracious host, was surprisingly able to supply the next lead. He recalled that G.G. worked at the post office, and he wasted no time calling him there. He got G.G., but the seeming culprit would say no more than that the car was not available.

It was October 7, exactly one month before the trial was scheduled to begin. The deadline was battering at Gene's patience. But, he wouldn't give up on G.G., so he thanked Paul and went to his sister's house on the other side of Eau Claire. This was no retreat. Gene had decided to confront Mr. G.G. He planned to take his brother-in-law, Ron Christner, along. "Ron is a big, burly chap who would be assuring to have at my side when confronting Mr. G.G. I had a strong feeling that I had 'a rat cornered' and that my day was about to be productive," Gene noted.

So, on that very same day, October 7, Gene Brotzman and the very large Ron Christner arrived at G.G.'s home at about 5 p.m. This confrontation was not exactly Odysseus coming home to face down 108 home wreckers and bad guys. Gene was about to face down one G.G., who turned out to be Mrs. Norbey's nephew. Was G.G. a willing villain or was he vulnerable? Was

97

he content to know the secret of Greenie's whereabouts or was the task of sustaining Mrs. Norbey's deception a burden he'd gladly lay down?

In the moment when sparks should have been flying, Fate softened the script. G.G. did not have a villain's monomania to drive him. Standing in his doorway face to face with Greenie's rightful owner, did he sense the jig was up... the milk was spilt... and surrender was the only way out? G.G. will ultimately turn out to be too nice to be a villain.

The Mystery of the Missing Classic

Part 3: The Recovery

The Mystery of the Missing Classic

Justice's deadline is approaching.

Chapter 9: In the Nick of Time

The Jig Is Up

"Gene, I'm glad you're here," said G.G., standing in his doorway in the late afternoon shadows on Saturday, October 7, 1978.

"I don't believe this!" said Gene to himself. He didn't believe he and his burly brother-in-law Ron—both loaded for bear and ready to confront a resister—would come face-to-face with a G.G. who was glad to see him. But, G.G. was in deep need of unburdening himself: "I tried to get my aunt to call you when the photo and ad came out in the Eau Claire paper and tell you to come and get the car, but she said no, that your ad would not locate the car and it would soon blow over."

"So Olga Norbey is at the bottom of this then," Gene replied.

"Yes, I've been storing the car for her. I even volunteered to take the car to you three weeks ago, but she would not hear of it. I've felt it wasn't right and wanted to get this over with. Olga is sick of it too, and would like to be done with it. She says she doesn't want the car anyway."

With the weight off his shoulders at last, G.G. tells Gene that he would like to contact Olga, who is at her cottage about 50 miles north of Eau Claire, to settle things. G.G. asks what Gene would want as a settlement so he could pass it on to Olga. Gene tells him that the least he would want in order to settle out of court is the car returned undamaged and payment for all the costs incurred in recovering the car, including attorney fees, reward money, advertising costs, etc. "Tomorrow," G.G. offers, "I'll call you tomorrow."

Justice Smiles on Sunday, October 8, 1978

Somehow it does seem appropriate that Greenie's redemption came on a Sunday. On that day Gene and his mom attended church together and then headed for Eau Claire. They lunched at the Fireside Steak House and went to sister Jackie's house for a meet-up to recover Greenie.

Gene took his sister Jackie, whose burly husband was out of town, plus Greg Nelson and Greg's first cous-

Chapter 9

in Barry Schultz to pick up the car at G.G.'s house. Unfortunately, nothing is easy in this case. Poor Greenie was not at G.G.'s house. She was hidden 50 miles north of Eau Claire back in the woods behind Olga's lakeside cabin. Greenie was hidden away in Chetek, a small village on a lake in Barron County, Wisconsin.

Pause for a moment and recall the woman who answered Gene's ad and told him she thought she saw the car in a parade in Barron? She could have been right, although Olga Norbey does not sound like a parade person. In fact, on this October day she still wanted to make it hard for Gene.

She and her husband LeRoy were supposed to bring the car to Eau Claire from its hiding place. When the Norbeys arrived at G.G.'s house they said they couldn't get a rig to haul the car so Gene couldn't get it that day. Gene recorded his response in his log of events:

> Of course another stall tactic! By this time I was feeling surges of anger and disgust. To keep from allowing any further stalling, I agreed to rent a truck and trailer from a relative in Eau Claire who was a mechanic and always had such equipment available for his business. ... When we returned to G.G.'s house, Mrs. Norbey emphatically informed us that we would not

103

be allowed to follow to get the car. That her nephew G.G. would drive the pickup. She was determined not to reveal where the car was stored or to implicate her cabin neighbors.

After laying down the law, the Norbeys left for their cabin. Gene and G.G. agreed that Olga had gone too far, and that Barry should drive the pick-up and trailer while G.G. accompanied him. It was a good arrangement, but they were about to encounter one last obstacle.

Greenie was stored in a secluded shed way back in the woods behind the Norbey's cabin. Barry had to proceed up a very narrow trail through the woods, jockeying around the overhanging branches to keep from scraping the truck. Unfortunately for Olga, the right side mirror on the pickup got bent and broken, and she would have to pay for the replacement. Once again, Gene recorded his response to what he felt was Mrs. Norbey's certainty that the car was safely hidden in her private woods.

> It never occurred to her that her most devious of deeds could or would ever be brought to light. I doubt that it ever occurred to her either that she would be made to pay every cent of cost her nasty deeds were adding up to,

Chapter 9

including the cost of replacing the mirror and bracket on the pick-up!

Wrapped in Deceit

At 7:50 p.m. on that same Sunday, October 8, 1978, Barry, G.G., and Greenie pulled up at Gene's sister's house where she, Gene, and Greg Nelson had been waiting and rejoicing. Racing out to greet the arrival, Gene discovered something loaded on the trailer that was wrapped tightly in canvas and secured by several lengths of rope.

It turns out that Mrs. Norbey had overseen the wrapping and loading of the car. Gene was certain that she had it wrapped to "keep secret the real Mrs. Olga Norbey's true nature and what she had been involved in." But it's possible—perhaps remotely possible—that she was not trying to hide her dastardly behavior, but instead meant to protect Greenie from getting scratched in the delivery. Should we grant her that much humanity?

Greenie at last made her appearance in a kind of automotive strip-tease as Barry and Greg carefully unwrapped her and loosened the tie-down ropes. With joy in his heart, Gene discovered the car had not been tampered with. She was still green with black fenders and yellow wire wheels. This was the moment of victory. Gene had beat the deadline of November 7, 1978

The Mystery of the Missing Classic

Greenie at last made her appearance in a kind of automotive strip-tease.

when the court would have denied him his ownership.

"I HAD WON! I HAD WON!!! Power, influence, wealth, position and knowing how to take advantage of someone had lost to a tenacious tenderfoot! If only my deceased wife could celebrate with me, then victory

Chapter 9

With the next day's light Gene took photos of Greenie, whose curvaceous lines were as beautiful as ever.

would be complete," Gene recorded.

Indeed, on Monday October 9, the day following this three-exclamation-point victory, Gene stopped on his way home to Edgerton and picked up the special gravestone he had ordered at Chippewa Falls Monument Company. "I was pleased with it as it did honor to my three-months-past departed wife," he noted.

On Wednesday, October 11, Gene brought Greenie home. It took until mid-November to straighten out paperwork releases and payments. Mrs. Norbey had agreed to pay all of Gene's expenses, including the $500 reward—which went to Paul Heebink, the young realtor who did so much to help locate Greenie in response

The Mystery of the Missing Classic

to Gene's ad.

The business was conducted by lawyer P., who had also encouraged Gene to sue and get more money than his expenses. "We have an airtight case," he said.

Lawsuit? More lawyer business? No dice. Gene knew his own mind:

> Mr. P., I'll stop you right there. There is no "we" at all in this case. You have totally failed me. All I got from you were letters, phone calls, bills, and discouragement. Mrs. Norbey will pay you what you have coming and that is the end of our relationship. Further, I have no desire to sue anyone. While Mrs. Norbey has engineered a terrible injustice to Greg Nelson and myself, I am not about to follow her example and do terrible things to her or anyone else. I have the coupe and all bills are being paid by Mrs. Norbey. Besides, I have learned some very valuable lessons in the whole process of getting the old coupe back to its rightful owner. Education is not cheap, but it is lasting. Consider this the end of this whole disgusting matter. Goodbye, Mr. P.

Greenie's advocate carefully filed a note of his words during that telephone call with lawyer P. in his records.

Chapter 9

One More Success

Some things never really end. Gene was told that Mrs. Norbey and her lawyer G. had put a restriction in the letter that accompanied their payment and release. They said no publicity could be pursued. They probably knew that Bill Stokes of the *Milwaukee Journal* was ready to print up the amazing little history of deceit. Gene could barely contain his outrage.

> Ha! Now attorney G. is trying to put a gag order on me. The audacity! Mrs. Norbey and Mr. G. are both on a banana peel and about to slip. I have the law on my side and they have been clearly caught in violation of several laws. Do they think I'm a total moron? Do they realize how fortunate they are that I haven't followed up with a hefty law suit exposing to all the world their dirty tricks?
>
> Yes, I will continue to be civil, considerate and polite. I will ask Bill Stokes to not use the real names of the violators, not because those two antagonists demand it that way, but because I choose to do it out of civility and a desire to have no further contact with them.

Those were the instructions Gene gave to the *Milwaukee Journal* columnist Bill Stokes. And the article

The Mystery of the Missing Classic

THE MILWAUKEE JOURNAL

—Journal Photo by Erwin Gebhard

Edgerton School Principal Gene Brotzman with the once lost 1932 Plymouth Coupe

Stokes

Little Green Car Found, at Last

From Page 1

up. She said that the car had "disappeared."

Settlement Refused

A judge said it appeared to be a case of abandonment and suggested that a $500 settlement be accepted by Brotzman. Brotzman did not look upon this as justice and a jury trial was set for Nov. 7, 1978.

Last September, while awaiting the trial, Brotzman ran a number of large ads in the Eau Claire Leader offering a $500 reward for information leading to the return of the Plymouth.

The ads carried a picture of the car and said, in part, "it was allegedly stolen from near Mrs. Norby's garage at one of her rental homes on 508½ Vine St."

In response to one of the ads, real estate dealer Barry Schultz contacted Brotzman and said he seen a car similar to Brotzman's Plymouth while soliciting a real estate listing some time ago.

With this information he went to Eau Claire and turned detective. The home where Schultz had seen the old car had changed hands and the new owner said yes there had been an antique car in the garage when he first moved there. But it had been removed and he did not know where it was.

Turns Detective

Then with sleuthing that would have done credit to Sherlock Holmes, Brotzman located the man who had allegedly moved the old car. The man denied ever having seen it.

Brotzman next located the previous owner of the home where the old car had been seen. When confronted with the information he had, the man said he knew where the old car was and would be relieved to return it to Brotzman. The man was a relative of Mrs. Norby's, he said.

Brotzman then contacted Mrs. Norby and said she too agreed that the car would be returned.

The car, it turned out, was hidden in the woods up near Chetek, and Brotzman provided a truck and trailer for Mrs. Norby's relative to go and haul it back to Eau Claire. Brotzman waited at his sister's home in Eau Claire and late on a Sunday afternoon the car was finally delivered, wrapped in pieces of old canvas, apparently to avoid the embarrassment that its identification might bring.

A Personal Victory

"It was a real personal victory," Brotzman said, "and I really regret that my wife could not have shared it with me."

Brotzman's wife died of cancer in August.

The little green car now sits in a garage at Brotzman's rural Edgerton home. The lawsuit Brotzman had filed has been dropped after a settlement was made. As a condition of the settlement, according to Brotzman's attorney, its terms cannot be publicized.

It is, however, a physical fact that Brotzman has his car and it is apparently safe to assume that he recovered his cost of finding it, including the $500 reward to Barry Schultz.

"It was a long period of real frustration," Brotzman said "and I am very glad that it is over."

The full story appeared in the Milwaukee Journal *on December 3, 1978 under the title "Little Green Car Finally Comes Home."*

Chapter 9

detailing the facts of the whole incident, with only a couple of them wrong, came out on the front page of the December 3, 1978 Sunday "Accent" section. The full story included a photo of Gene smiling alongside our girl Greenie under the title "Little Green Car Finally Comes Home."

Gene had tried, but guess what... Stokes did not change the names. He used the real ones. So did the *Eau Claire Leader-Telegram* when that paper printed the story under the slightly self-serving title "Ads Lead to Return of 'Missing' Antique Car." Hold your breath now, here comes the consequences from Mrs. Norbey and lawyer G.:

"Nothing, none, not a peep!" as Gene put it.

Apparently they knew they were in a bad position and a public dispute over the facts would only make it worse for them. Unfortunately, one person did get upset by seeing his name connected to Norbey's sordid mess—the man with the changed heart, G.G. As Barry Schultz, Gene's first cousin-in-law, spoke of it briefly in his otherwise cheerful Christmas letter to Gene. He ended the letter by saying, "It sure is good to know that the car is back in the family again where it belongs."

Reflections on a Two-Year Chase

Gene told lawyer P. that he had learned some les-

The Mystery of the Missing Classic

sons, although he doesn't list them anywhere. But, what have we to reflect on in this whole matter?

First, let's talk about "coincidences," because there is one more unusual connection to ponder. Gene's first cousin-in-law Barry Schultz and Mrs. Norbey's nephew G.G. drove the recovery truck together. Strangely enough these two also worked together in the same post office without knowing anything about each other's involvement in the case of the missing classic. They found out on the very day they sat side-by-side in the pick-up truck—just as they often worked side-by-side in the post office. "One chance in many million," Gene thought. Imagine what they must have talked about driving the pick-up to put right an injustice.

In any case, looking back over all the help Gene got—from people answering ads, friends and relations with connections, people with trucks and with time to help—it sounds like a wonderful chain of coincidences. But perhaps it was just small-town dynamics; perhaps in Eau Claire everyone is connected by only one degree of separation, rather than the fabled six degrees.

We can also reflect on Mrs. Norbey's motives. They seem inscrutable, opaque, and even irrational. Was it mere nastiness that drove her? Have you ever heard of "motiveless malignancy"? It's a term often used to describe Shakespeare's villain Iago in the play *Othello*.

Chapter 9

Some people just like to spoil things, no reason necessary. Beyond that, Mrs. Norbey's folly deepened with every opportunity she had to make amends.

Then there's the matter of advertising being more effective than lawyers. That's almost too comical to think about. And yet the slowness and actual injustice that dogged this case is a bit scary—as is the power of advertising.

Finally, we might think a bit about the value of dogged persistence. Neither injustice, disillusionment with the law, loss of a loved one, nor fatigue with two years of deception stopped Greenie's advocate, Gene Brotzman, from pursuing her restoration. But the story is not quite over. Greenie has been restored to her rightful owner—now she needs to be restored to her original glory. And that means Gene will have to do a lot more chasing around to find the parts and accessories that made the 1932 Plymouth PA the historic classic it is.

The Mystery of the Missing Classic

Ken Stadele delivers the restored classic in 1988.

Chapter 10: The Advocate's Last Challenge— Restoration

"Restoration is a journey."
—*Ken Stadele, President, Ken's Klassics, Inc.*

How a Car Restoration Becomes a Journey

Any good journey story involves a search, a discovery, and a return or recovery. Greenie's advocate, Gene Brotzman became a fully committed searcher. He did the legwork to find authentic parts—and he did it both before he teamed up with a professional restoration facility and after. It took some sleuthing to complete the restoration and a lot of detailed searching.

We can't go on every leg of that search, but fortunately Gene recorded details of one incident in his pursuit of parts—his hunt for the exactly correct headlights. We can read it as one example of what added up to truly dedicated efforts in restoring the 1932 Plymouth PA Rumble Seat Coupe to her proper splendor.

Prior to the beginning of the professional restoration, I was able to locate some desired parts at the Iola, Wisconsin annual Old Car Show and Swap Meet held each July. Here is how I came upon a pair of good, restorable headlights that are original equipment for a 1932 PA Plymouth.

The Iola Old Car Show and Swap Meet is a very large place with several thousand vendors. The only means of transportation up and down row after row of vendors is by walking. ... After steady walking for nearly a day, I came upon a vendor who had, among his several other types of ware, some old headlight shells (buckets). I asked the vendor if any of them would be for a '32 PA Plymouth. Here my luck began to change. He had only one, and was anxious to sell it. Naturally I bought it with a smile, realizing that now at least I know just what shape the headlights should be.

So I carried the bucket with me as I continued my walk. This was on a Friday. The next day, I continued my walk down row upon row

Chapter 10

of vendors whom I had not gotten to the previous day. Carrying the headlight bucket with me, I continued to scan each vendor space, hoping for a miracle. Unexpectedly a deep voice called out to me, "Hey, whatcha got there? Looks like a Plymouth headlight bucket!" I was all too quick to agree that, "Yes, it is for a Plymouth." The owner of the deep voice responded with, "Come here, I think I have what you are looking for!" My steps quickened and so did my breath.

The vendor produced a complete pair of headlights for a 1931–32 PA Plymouth. They were in good restorable condition with buckets, reflector shells, electric sockets for the bulbs, glass, and chrome rings to hold the glass in place. Wow! What a feeling of elation. Needless to say, I did not dicker on the price. I promptly paid the vendor, thanking him repeatedly for being so sharp and observant to notice what I was carrying.

Now my goal for the trip to Iola was met and my feet were tired. I took my plastic bag of "gold" and headed for the car. After all of that walking, I relished the soft seat of my car. On the way home I kept marveling at the good fortune

I had just encountered. A stroke of good luck was really what I had just experienced. Maybe, just maybe, my luck would continue to be good and finding restoration parts would not be that difficult. The reality of it was that it turned out not to be that difficult to locate parts, but very time-consuming.

"Not too difficult," he said. Well, if you enjoy reading "motorhead" details, take a look at Appendix A to see an abridged list of the sources Gene consulted and what he got from them. Long as that list is, it's still far from the whole story. Impassioned searchers frequently find themselves slogging through what would be tedious to read about, but is actually part of their journey to completion—as exciting to them as the tension in a tightly matched, fast-paced ball game. Get the idea? Good. Now let's trace the stages of Greenie's restoration, starting from the beginning.

Back to the Beginning
Stage One: The Early Efforts

Gene Brotzman undertook some restorations of his own between the time he recovered Greenie in 1978 and the time he turned the car over to the professionals at Ken's Klassics, Inc. of Muscoda, Wisconsin, in 1987.

Chapter 10

The tangled beginning of a restoration journey ...

... And the journey's satisfying conclusion, as Ken Stadele delivers the restored Greenie to Gene Brotzman.

The Mystery of the Missing Classic

> **Note:** In the interim between 1978 and 1987, Gene resigned his job as an elementary school principal shortly after his first wife's heartbreaking, early death. He took a job with the Neuendorf Trucking Company. He later returned to education. He also took a second wife, Barbara M. Hoyum.

Here's how Gene's records describe some of his early efforts.

> From the time the car was delivered into my possession in 1978, until my wife Barbara and I decided it was time to have the car professionally restored in 1987, I used the *Plymouth Bulletins* along with *Hemmings Motor News* to begin to locate parts that I knew were a priority.
>
> One of the first was the Flying Lady radiator cap which was the main defining feature of the '32 Plymouth. I located a new old stock (NOS) Flying Lady through an ad in the *Plymouth Owners Club Bulletin*. While it was the correct one, it failed to stop the leakage. Later on I found the reason was the radiator shroud was shimmed too high, prohibiting the radiator cap from sealing tightly.

Chapter 10

Greenie gets her first taste of weddings.

I had a retired mechanic, Louie Handel of Mazomanie, Wisconsin, restore the brake wheel and master cylinders so the car was drivable.

Gene searched out a great many more improvements and even got to show off Greenie a bit, as he describes in his records.

Before the car was restored in the 1980s, I detailed the coupe with much "elbow grease," cleaning and polishing the car to the point that I could say to my wife, "It's ready to be used at your sister Karen's wedding. I will pick them

The Mystery of the Missing Classic

up out front after the wedding ceremony. They can get into the rumble seat, and while they wave goodbye to the crowd gathered on the steps, I will slowly drive away." Turns out that is just the way it worked out.

Greenie's preliminary debut at this wedding was dramatic, romancing the crowds by motoring off with the young honeymoon-bound couple tucked in the rumble seat. But that's just a foretaste of Greenie's grand successes to come.

Stage Two: Assessing the Dimensions of the Challenge

On August 28, 1987 Gene turned the car over to Ken's Klassics for what turned out to be a nine-month "frame-up, body-off professional restoration." The first step in that process was to do an inventory of what was there and what was missing.

Parts Missing

Radiator cap, crank hole cover, left front hubcap, left door outside handle, interior window molding on the driver's door, step plates on running boards, rear oval window crank, vacuum tank for reserve vacuum for the windshield wiper, rumble seat side panels, luggage rack, right side tail light and bracket, gear shift knob,

Chapter 10

METICULOUS PARTIAL OR TOTAL RESTORATION OF ALL MODELS OF ANTIQUE, CLASSIC, AND SPECIAL INTEREST AUTOMOBILES

Ken's Klassics

ON HWY. 60, ½ MILE WEST OF HWY. 80
ROUTE ONE, MUSCODA, WISCONSIN 53573
PHONE 608 739-4242

CERTIFICATE OF RECEIPT

Be it known that on the 28th day of August, 1987, Mr. Ken Stadele, owner of Ken's Klassics, Muscoda, WI 53573, received one 1932 Plymouth Model PA Rumble Seat Coupe, Vehicle Identification Number 161944, Engine Number PA52829, from Mr. Gene Brotzman, 28 Appleby Circle, Mazomanie, WI 53560.

Be it also known that the above stated vehicle was received by Ken's Klassics to undergo restoration as discussed by Mr. Ken Stadele and Mr. Gene Brotzman.

A prepayment of services of $ 0.00 was also received on this 28th day of August, 1987.

Ken Stadele
Ken Stadele

KEN STADELE, OWNER - MEMBER OF
AUBURN · CORD · DUESENBERG CLUB • THE PACKARD CLUB • PACKARDS INTERNATIONAL MOTOR CAR CLUB
INTERNATIONAL SOCIETY FOR VEHICLE PRESERVATION • ANTIQUE AUTOMOBILE CLUB OF AMERICA • PLUS OTHERS

On August 28, 1987 Gene turned the car over to Ken's Klassics for professional restoration.

gas pedal knob, fuel pump heat shield, and a spare tire mounting bracket.

Poor Replacements

Besides all of the missing parts, there were many substitute parts, which were not the original type for the car. The headlights were Model A Ford after-market replicas, the horn was mounted outside on the headlight crossbar in front of the radiator (it should be mounted under the hood on the engine block). Directional lights were over-the-counter plastic, and were not standard equipment in 1932. The front bumper was from a vintage Chevrolet. The hubcaps were original, but badly damaged and deteriorated. One of the two side-mount spare tires was an old original knobby used for winter driving and did not match the other tires. The single taillight was an over-the-counter plastic type, the window glass on the driver's side was cracked, the interior seat covers and rumble seat cover were black Naugahyde, and the door trim panels were of the same black material.

Inoperable Functions

Here is a partial listing of what was wrong with the car: The gas and fuel gauges did not work at all, the windshield wiper (there is only one) did not work, the brake fluid constantly oozed out of the master cylinder and the wheel cylinders, making the brakes highly unreliable. The emergency brake had very little holding power, the radiator cap did not fit tightly enough to stop radiator fluid from bubbling out around it, and the tires were cracked and in need of replacing.

Ken's Klassics could find some of the parts, and knew where to send parts for rebuilding and how to address inoperable functions. But to move the process along, Gene continued to be the chief parts locator for scarce and difficult-to-find parts.

Stages Three through Nine

Gene clearly articulated what he wanted for Greenie: "My goal for the '32 Plymouth PA coupe was to end up with a striking and eye-catching antique car that is proper (original parts) in every way and safe and reliable to drive."

In pursuit of that goal, Ken's Klassics provided nine detailed monthly reports on the progress of the restoration—nine lengthy entries for Greenie's diary. Let's begin by looking at the first report in November 1987 concerning work done in October. It sets the pattern for the next nine months.

The reports ran from 9 to 15 pages. Each was really a formatted package of information, each with the same organizational structure. They begin with a narrative letter organized to give a brief overview of the month and a brief explanation of each of the attached standard monthly enclosures. Each month the enclosures included:

- a monthly bill statement;
- a detailed labor report;
- a lengthy list of supplies used;
- a list of parts received from Gene Brotzman; and
- a lengthy list of what was done—parts and labor.

Sounds dry, but if you read it as a car lover might, you'll find an emotional subtext that will slowly take hold of you. You might find you can read those monthly reports as if you were reading Greenie's diary—the running story of her makeover, her restored good looks, and her remade vitality.

Here, as an example, is the opening narrative overview taken from Ken's first report on November 5, 1987.

> Enclosed are your billing statements for the month of October. As you can see by the detailed labor report the chemically stripped parts were picked up on October 2, 1987. A photograph of these parts has been enclosed for your reference. Numerous close-up shots of the rust

Chapter 10

Gene Brotzman - 1932 Plymouth - Billing

Month of January - Page 3

Date	Part or Amount of Labor	Price	Total
	Balance brought forward		2,116.04
1/25/88	7 3/4 hours labor (install right and left running boards, wetsand right and left front fenders and right rear fender, wetsand right side of cowl and roof, repaint rumble seat lid, buff right and left front fenders, right door, left and right rear quarters and right rear fenders)	155.00	2,321.04
1/26/88	7½ hours labor (wetsand roof and rumble seat lid, buff front and rear fenders, doors, cowl, roof, and rear quarters, bolt down body, install cowl lacing and windshield gasket)	145.00	2,466.04
1/27/88	Shipping on parts purchased from F. Andrews on January 20th, 1988	8.13	2,474.17
	7 3/4 hours labor (paint radiator, spare tire holders, work on luggage rack and sandblast, install side mount supports, disasssemble outer door handles, box up door handles and window cranks for shipping)	155.00	2,629.17
1/28/88	UPS shipping charges - shipped out items for chrome plating	1.63	2,630.80
1/29/88	Woodgraining includes UPS shipping and COD charges	502.79	3,133.59
	Supplies used week of 1/25/88 to 1/29/88 - see invoice for complete breakdown -	29.73	3,163.32

This billing is complete and up to date as of January 31st, 1988. If full payment of this invoice is not received or postmarked by the 10th of February, interest will be charged at 1½% per month. Thank you.

Monthly reports provided the running story of Greenie's makeover.

The Mystery of the Missing Classic

damaged areas were also taken. You will see that there are some actual rust-through holes on some of the body panels.

As you will see the front and rear shocks have been received. A copy of the letter requesting the work done is enclosed for your records. The restored radiator emblem has also been received. A list of weatherstrips needed for your car has been developed and we will be ordering these items in the near future.

Ken's process included a running interaction with Gene. Each month Ken listed all the parts he received from Gene in separate enclosures. In the first month's report (the one we've been reviewing) Ken received a total of seven parts from Gene, and requested Gene's help with the color scheme:

"Despite our attempts we have not been able to locate paint chips for your car. Do you have a color scheme already in mind? Please contact me so that we can discuss this phase of the restoration further."

Gene's Color Choices

In response to Ken's request Gene did his usual research and made the color choices for the interior and exterior body finish.

Chapter 10

Rather than a painted dash and inside window trim, I chose to have these surfaces wood-grained. That type of finish makes the interior of the vehicle look rich and professional. Further, after consultation with Frank Andrews of Pennsylvania and Robert McMulkin of New York state, I chose a paint scheme that is unusual but meets all of the requirements of those who judge antique cars. The wire wheels will be vermilion, the main body French silver grey acrylic lacquer, the fenders, rocker panels, wide strip of accent on the sides to be Copra Drab Poly acrylic lacquer, with vermilion pin-striping.

During the writing of this book, as Gene reflected back on his decisions, he approved of what he saw: "This choice proved to be a good one. Many compliments are heard when the car is out in the public. One lady was heard saying, 'Wow, isn't that sharp? I would rate this car the best of show.'"

Together the monthly reports add up to a story of tiny parts and big connections, patience and day-to-day rededication. Here's a brief collage of blood, sweat, and tears taken over nine months:

> The front and rear shocks are here...the clutch and pressure plate showed considerable wear

and were sent out for rebuilding...front engine mounts, the front bumper, generator and wheel cylinder dust caps were ordered...the chrome plating was received from the platers who had a lot of problems plating the grill shell as it was in such poor condition...the water temperature gauge and face were shipped out for restoration...all of the door handles received from you were sent to F. Andrews and he was able to determine which were correct and sell us those that were needed to make a complete set...the battery support plate, inside rear view mirror assembly and rear center bumper bolt were ordered.

That's the way a journey goes, taking step by muddy step through sloughs of despond and fields of clover.

Ken's Summary

At the end of the restoration, in 1988, Ken provided Gene with an official appraisal of Greenie's value, and in doing so, conveyed a concise—but a little spare—overview of the restoration stages:

> [The restoration consisted of:] chemically stripping the body of paint, proper body and metal working, restoration of suspension parts, rebuilt carburetor and fuel pump, relined brakes,

Chapter 10

A beauty restored and professionally photographed for her debut by Glatch Productions of Wauwatosa.

new brake hoses and lines, new weatherstrips, rebuilt shocks, new wiring harness, resurfaced clutch and pressure plate, woodgrained interior mouldings, powder coated rims, restored and rebuilt dash gauges, rechromed front and rear bumpers, new upholstery, new wood bows in roof, and a hand rubbed Copra Drab and French Silver Grey lacquer paint job.

Using the appropriate authoritative references, Ken valued the car in 1988 at "approximately $20,000 to $22,500." We won't mention what Greenie's advocate paid to get her ready for that assessment.

At Journey's End

Searchers frequently arrive back where they started, having learned the depth and meaning of what they sought. Gene had plumbed human nature in his encounter with Mrs. Norbey, and then he had to travel a rocky road toward restoring princess Greenie to her throne. But in the end, he got to see Greenie, no longer green, but otherwise back fully to her own beginnings.

To witness Greenie's post-restoration activities and follow her trail of adoration, turn to the Epilogue.

Epilogue: Leaving a Trail of Classic Delight—Greenie's New Life

In 2009 Ken's Klassics still restores vintage vehicles in Muscoda, Wisconsin—and T.J. Krueger is still assisting Ken Stadele, as he did with Greenie's restoration in 1987.

The Mystery of the Missing Classic

Although Ken Stadele of Ken's Klassics asked Greenie's advocate, Gene Brotzman, to decide if he wanted a car to travel on today's highways or a "parade car," he actually was suggesting there was no real choice. "These older cars are not designed for today's highway speeds. You wouldn't be happy with the way it would ride, or the way it handles, or the speed it can go. What you have is a parade car," Ken reported to Gene. To be true to Greenie's original capacities, she would have to be used gently—a parade car exists to share glory with its riders. And that is exactly what is happening to Greenie in her new life.

After her completed restoration, Greenie has been shepherded about by Gene and his wife, Barb. Greenie leaves a trail of good feelings, fond memories, and genuine pleasure wherever she goes. She even got to transport the parade marshal in an annual Sauk City "Cow Chip" parade. The parade marshal was Craig Culver, who with his wife, Lea Culver, owns the Culver's chain of restaurants. The couple rode proudly in Greenie's stately rumble seat.

Among the weddings and other events where Greenie has stolen the show, Gene recorded two particular incidents that reflect Gene and Greenie's delightful partnership in good will.

Epilogue

Greenie transported the parade marshal in an annual Sauk City "Cow Chip" parade.

In one wedding, the ceremony was to be in the yard of Rachel Accola's parents' home. To get to the location, one had to drive up a rather steep driveway, which passes over a crown in the landscape just before arriving at the yard location. I had the bride with me down the hill out of sight near some buildings. Using walkie-talkies, my wife gave me the signal as to when to begin driving the bride up the hill to the wedding site.

I had spent some time rehearsing with Rachel just how to get into the rumble seat, and how to get out. The wedding attendees were all seated, waiting for the bride to appear. They had no idea as to just what was in store for them. They could not see down the road because of a crown in the landscape.

The faint hum of the '32 Plymouth's 4-cylinder engine began to register in the ears of the gathering. Then gradually appearing over the crown was first the nose with the Flying Lady radiator cap followed by the shiny chrome radiator shell, the "big eyes" headlights, and then the rest of the car.

In all of her elegance, the bride smiled from the rumble seat of the graceful old car. As the coupe came to a halt, it was time for the bride to "dismount" from her perch in the rumble seat.

"Let's see, you step out first with your right foot?!" I was right there in my tux with a hand held out to assist Rachel. Rather than stepping out with her right foot and facing the front of the car, she sought to start out with her left foot and descend facing the rear of the coupe. This will never do. She would get her feet tangled up and stumble with dozens of pairs of eyes watching every move!

Epilogue

An elegant bride enjoys transport to her outdoor wedding in an elegant car.

Needless to say, I had to ask Rachel to back up and start over. Now she was over her panic and was listening to me and remembering what we had rehearsed. She backed up and promptly proceeded to dismount gracefully as she had rehearsed. What a relief. Now the groom stepped forward to take her by the hand and the service was off to a good start.

That was one of Greenie's many contributions to romance and to the big events in young people's lives. But she shone even more as a memory provocateur, an aide to nostalgia, a mirror for sweet tears. Here's Gene's

The Mystery of the Missing Classic

account of one such event when Greenie took some guests on a trip down memory lane.

> One particularly rewarding day for me was when I took the '32 Plymouth coupe to the Pines Manor in Prairie du Sac, Wisconsin. I was to play a 45-minute harmonica concert for the old folks and then those who were able could come out by the front entrance and take a walk around the '32 coupe. That should give them a flood of memories of their early days and the accompanying experiences. A group of the old patriarchs gathered in a circle around me.
>
> As I played all of the oldies with which they were familiar, some of them burst into croaky singing, some just tapped their toes. Several of the dear old souls sat in wheel chairs with their heads on their chests and body slumped over. Surely they were sleeping. But wait, in spite of all of the signs of sleep, I noted with pleasure that they, too, were keeping time with their feet! What a surprise.
>
> As I continued the concert, several made requests for their favorite songs. Each time a request was played, invariably there would be some singing. What a pleasure to do some-

Epilogue

A 102-year-old-man felt comfortable visiting with vintage Greenie.

thing for others that brings them pleasure, but that also brings you the great reward of your own satisfaction.

After the concert, attendants came and wheeled the wheel chairs with their occupants to the front entrance to see the old car. The compliments came quickly:

"We had a car just like this except it had four doors."

"I've ridden in that little back seat [rumble seat] many times."

"The first car I ever owned was a Ford coupe."

"Has this car always looked so nice?"

If the car could talk, I'm sure the compliments heard would bring an "aaa-oo-ga" from the horn.

Some of the old folks passed their hands along the smooth lines of the old car. Some looked at themselves in the reflection from the headlight buckets. All showed great pleasure in seeing the old car. As I loaded the coupe back into it's enclosed trailer, I couldn't help but smile when I recalled how much pleasure I had experienced, not because of anything I had done or received, but of the reactions from the residents. I shall do it again upon invitation.

So the mystery of the missing classic closes with sunbeams illuminating a lovely old car—a bit tarted up in French Grey—but now the host of a new mystery: Why is she still called Greenie?

The End

Epilogue

Barb and Gene Brotzman enjoying Greenie's company.

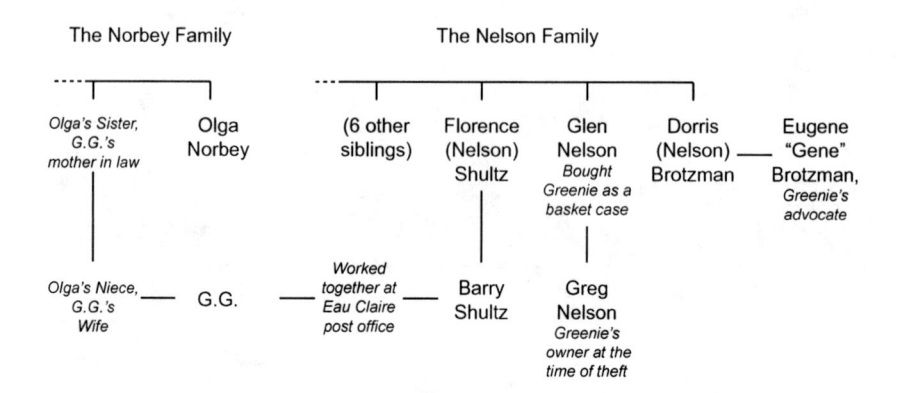

The Mystery of the Missing Classic

The Norbey Family

- Olga's Sister, G.G.'s mother in law
- Olga Norbey

- Olga's Niece, G.G.'s Wife — G.G.

The Nelson Family

- (6 other siblings)
- Florence (Nelson) Shultz
- Glen Nelson — *Bought Greenie as a basket case*
- Dorris (Nelson) Brotzman
- Eugene "Gene" Brotzman, *Greenie's advocate*

- Worked together at Eau Claire post office
- Barry Shultz
- Greg Nelson — *Greenie's owner at the time of theft*

Appendix I: Relationships

1. Gene Brotzman—ultimate owner of Greenie from 1976 to present
2. Greg Nelson—son of Glenn Nelson and owner of the car-napped car from 1967 to 1976
3. Glenn Nelson—owner of Greenie from 1964 to 1967 and father of Greg Nelson
4. Mrs. Olga Norbey—the landlady who car-napped Greenie in 1974
5. Lawyer P.—Gene Brotzman's attorney
6. Lawyer G.—Mrs. Norbey's attorney
7. Judge B.—judge assigned to the missing car case
8. Paul Heebink—provider of the winning clue
9. G.G.—temporary keeper of the car-napped Plymouth; nephew of Mrs. Norbey

The Mystery of the Missing Classic

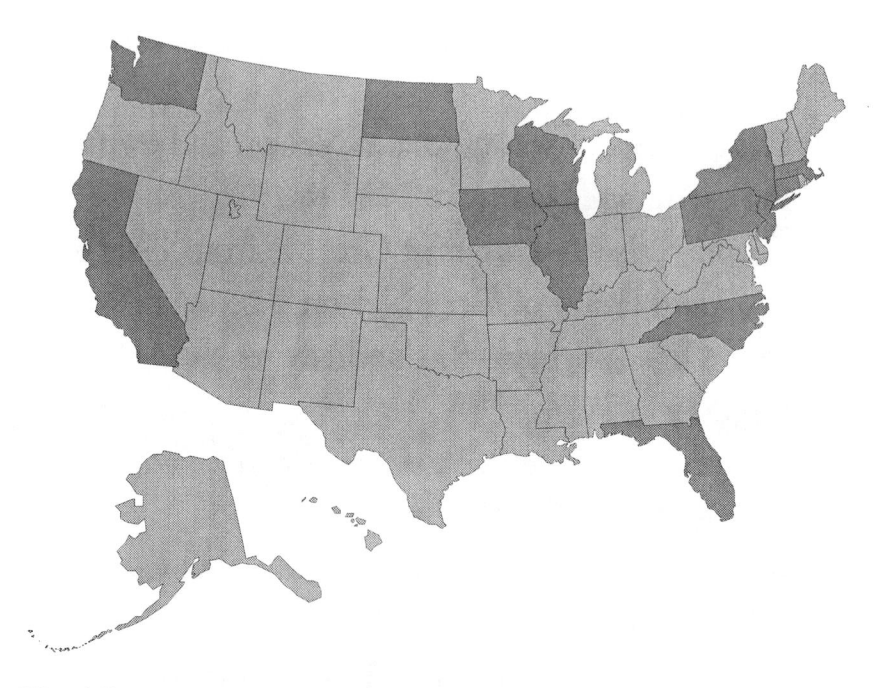

The following states provided parts and information: Arkansas, California, Connecticut, Florida, Illinois, Iowa, Massachusetts, New Jersey, New York, North Carolina, North Dakota, Pennsylvania, Washington, and Wisconsin.

Appendix II: Sources for Parts and Information

Gene Brotzman and Ken Stadele faced a considerable challenge in locating parts and information about the 1932 PA Plymouth Rumble Seat Coupe. That specific model was only in production for a short time. The PA designation identified these Plymouths as 1931 and 1932 production years. In the spring of 1932, minor changes were made and from that date forward the Plymouths were referred to as the PB series.

Parts and information came from a minimum of 14 states. Several other sources were not recorded, especially those suppliers used prior to the full restoration process.

Many national contacts for parts came from *Hemmings Motor News*, the largest and oldest magazine catering to collectors of antique, classic, and exotic sports cars. After Gene Brotzman got into the parts retrieval process, he began to get referrals from various suppliers who knew of others who had various rare parts available.

The Mystery of the Missing Classic

Parts/information sought:	Parts/information provided by:
New upholstery	Al's Auto Interiors S12626 Donald Rd, Route 2 Spring Green, WI 53588
Converted the luggage rack from a sedan to a coupe, rechromed the door handle he sold. "A gold mine of information," said Gene Brotzman.	Frank Andrews Hillegass Rd Pennsburg, PA 18073
Samples of upholstery fabric and number of pleats needed.	Harry Baker Mason City, Iowa
Restored carburetor	Beneke & Culver 1217 Culmen off Regent St. Madison, WI
Throttle and choke knobs. Information.	Floyd Carlstrom Madison, WI
Points, condenser, rotor and rotor cap	Component Parts, Ltd 1387 Brighton-Henrietta Tn Ln Rd. Rochester, NY 14623
Owner's Manual	Crank and Hope Publications
Chrome plating of headlight buckets, etc.	Custom Chrome Plating, Inc. 963 Mechanic St. Grafton, OH 44044
Door sill plates and temp gauge	Andrew Edler 4053 Leo's Lane Carmichael, CA 95608
Parking brake lining	Eggeman Truck Madison, WI
Set of side-mount tire mirrors with straps	Jay Fisher Acken Drive 4B Clark, NJ 07066
Transmission mount and other parts.	Tom Hanaford Antique Auto Parts Cellar, Box 3 South Weymouth, MA 02190
Maintenance work	Louie Handel 14 South Johns St. Mazomanie, WI 53560
Pair of headlights plus other parts	Iola Old Car Show and Swap Mt. Iola, WI

Appendix II

Parts/information sought:	Parts/information provided by:
Restored gas tank	Judd's Radiator Service, Inc. 1401 South Park St. Madison, WI 53715
Repaired wheel lugs	Mike Kohlman Ent. Sauk City, WI
Gaskets	Gerald J. Lettieri 132 Old Main St. Rocky Hill, CN 70606
Information and parts list	Ronald Mac Kenzie 4648 W. 98th St. Oak Lawn, Illinois 60453
Luggage rack, tail lights, running boards "As a national consultant to the *Plymouth Bulletin* for '31 & '32. Plymouths, Mac Kenzie was a great help for information and parts," said Gene Brotzman.	Robert McMulkin 210 Harrison Ave. Miller Place, NY 11764
Repaired distributor	Wayne Moen Greenway Cross to Stewart St. Madison, WI
Manifold gasket information	Mitchell Motor Parts 1037 Parson's Ave. Columbus, Ohio 43206
Tie downs for hauling '32 Plymouth	M&R Products 2979 S. Delsea Dr. Vineland, NJ 08360
6 new hubcaps	NC Industries, Inc. 215 S. Thomas Ave. Sayre, PA 18840
Manifold gasket	Olson's Gaskets Box 242 Manchester, WA. 98353
Many contacts; Flying Lady radiator cap	The Plymouth Owners Club, Inc. Box 416 Cavalier, ND 58220-0416
Car cover	Reliable Motoring Accessories 1751-H7 Spruce St. Riverside, CA 92507

147

The Mystery of the Missing Classic

Parts/information sought:	Parts/information provided by:
Running board rubber	Restoration Specialists & Supply, Inc. P. O. Box 328 Windber, PA 15963 814-467-9842
Information	Clarence Schlicht 1646 Kane Ave. La Crosse, WI 54603
Tires and tubes	Sears and Roebuck & Co.
Restore radiator & vacuum lines.	Suburban Motors, Inc. 1110 State St. Black Earth, WI 53534
Insurance since 1979	J.C. Taylor, Inc. 320 South 69th St. Upper Darby, PA 19082
Restore Temperature gauge	The Temperature Gauge Guy 521 Wood St. Dunedin, FL 33528
lug nuts	Ed Thompson 134 East 219th St. Euclid, OH 44123
Fan blade	Duane L. Vaudt Box 184 Clear Lake, IA 50428
Floor mat	Pat Walsh, Auto Parts, Inc. 39 Bartley St. Wakefield, MA 01880
Gas hose & filter	Weaver Auto Parts
Wheel studs	Mazomanie & Madison, WI
Amp gauge and fuel tank sending unit	Williamson Instrument Highway 282 Chester, AR 72901
Information	Roger Winstanley 324 fdsN 76th St. Milwaukee, WI 53222
Restore gauges	John Wolf & Co. 4741 Sherwin Rd. Willoughby, OH 44094
Information	Gene Ziells Evansville, WI

About the Author

After 38 years as an elementary school principal followed by 18 years of retirement, author Gene Brotzman felt the true account of what happened in the mid 1970s to the Little Green Car called "Greenie" had to be told.

Here is a story of just how deceptive and dishonest people can be. Is it possible that an innocent-looking 72-year-old lady would have the audacity to steal an antique car?

The author went to the legal system for help in locating and retrieving his beloved 1932 Plymouth Rumble Seat Coupe. This was the biggest mistake Gene made in trying to clear up this whole disturbing mess. The two lawyers he engaged to locate the missing classic did nothing but make phone calls, write letters, and send bills based on their billable hours. Nothing was accomplished. Meanwhile the clock was ticking and the car still missing. Depositions were held. The judge who reviewed the deposition tape came back with a recommendation that will literally knock your socks off!

The Mystery of the Missing Classic

The author was unable to convince the lawyers or the judge to allow their names to be used in this tale of deception. So, the lawyers are referred to only by a letter, as Lawyer P., Lawyer G. and Lawyer H. The judge is referred to in the same way, Judge B. And one other participant in this tale goes only by G.G.

So just how do you solve a theft if the legal system has failed you miserably? Here is the story of how a novice but very determined Gene Brotzman took the bull by the horns and tackled the unsolvable *Mystery of the Missing Classic*.

The author is available for personal appearances
with Greenie the 1932 Plymouth Rumble Seat Coupe.
Contact Eugene Brotzman at 608-643-0717 or
brotzman1035@verizon.net.

To order more copies of this book,
use the order form on the following page.

Share **The Mystery of the Missing Classic** with other lovers of mysteries and classic cars.

Just call 608-643-0717 or send us this order form with your payment.

The Mystery of the Missing Classic
by Eugene Brotzman

...a *"can't put it down"* true story!

How did the "sweet" old granny pull it off? And why didn't the legal system stop her? The story of "Greenie" the *1932 Plymouth Rumble Seat Coupe* will blow your gaskets!

PLEASE PRINT   Today's Date _____

Your Name _____

Address _____

City/State/ZIP _____

E-mail _____

Quantity: _____ *The Mystery of the Missing Classic* @ $14.95 = _____
Ship to: ☐ Same as above   Shipping: _____
                5% Sales Tax if WI resident: _____
                    Total Amt. Enclosed: _____

If shipping to a different address:

Recipient's Name _____

Address _____

City/State/ZIP _____

| Shipping: $5.25 first book $4.00 each add'l book | Mail payment with order form to: Eugene Brotzman 1035 20th Street Prairie du Sac, WI 53578 |